Moving the Chains

Moving the Chains

*An Operational Solution for
Embracing Complexity in the
Digital Age*

Domenico Lepore

BEP BUSINESS EXPERT PRESS

Moving the Chains: An Operational Solution for Embracing Complexity in the Digital Age

Copyright © Business Expert Press, LLC, 2019.

First published in 2019 by
Business Expert Press, LLC
222 East 46th Street, New York, NY 10017
www.businessexpertpress.com

ISBN-13: 978-1-94897-620-6 (paperback)
ISBN-13: 978-1-94897-621-3 (e-book)

Business Expert Press Supply and Operations Management Collection

Collection ISSN: 2156-8189 (print)
Collection ISSN: 2156-8200 (electronic)

Cover and interior design by Exeter Premedia Services Private Ltd., Chennai, India

First edition: 2019

10 9 8 7 6 5 4 3 2 1

Printed in the United States of America.

To my wife, Angela.
We are one.

Abstract

Our world is increasingly digital and decentralized. We must therefore urgently rethink, structurally and operationally, how organizations are designed so they can adapt and compete in the digital age. This starts by understanding the problems raised by complexity.

Complexity, i.e., a reality that is highly interconnected and interdependent, is forcing organizations to experience an inherent conflict. They must protect the fundamental needs of accountability and growth and this can no longer be done through a traditional hierarchical/functional structure with its resulting silos, nor by abandoning hierarchy completely. The way out of this conflict is to acknowledge that an organization is

(a) A network
(b) Part of a larger network of value

Managing an organization as a network entails forgoing a command and control management style but at the same time requires a powerful mechanism to ensure that activities are properly coordinated and everybody in the network is accountable.

We can find a suitable organizational structure if we look at the fundamental elements that make up the work of an organization. Just as the key constituents of life are hydrogen, oxygen, carbon, nitrogen, phosphorus, and sulfur, we can say that the basic constituents of work are *repetitive processes* and *one-off projects*.

A new organizational design emerges that is based on the management of a complex, strongly interconnected *network of projects*.

What propels the performance of such a network are low variation processes and a finite capacity-based algorithm that allows a realistic allocation of available resources from a pool of competencies. This requires a complete shift from a "mechanical" mindset to a systemic one to overcome the command and control management style in favor of whole system optimization.

Designing organizations as networks of projects equips them structurally, operationally, and cognitively to optimize their interactions with larger networks of value through digital and decentralized transactions.

Keywords

Decentralized; digitization; complexity; organization design; network of projects; variation; W. Edwards Deming; Theory of Profound Knowledge; Theory of Constraints; systemic management; Future of Work; Collaboration; Project Management; Critical Chain; Network Thinking; Leadership; Management

Contents

What is most magnificent about human invention is how we open for ourselves new conceptions of reality previously unimaginable.

——Rabbi Menachem Mendel Schneerson,
Likutei Sichos vol. 15, pp. 42–48

The most beautiful emotion we can experience is the mystical. It is the power of all true art and science. He to whom this emotion is a stranger, who can no longer wonder and stand rapt in awe, is as good as dead. To know that what is impenetrable to us really exists, manifesting itself as the highest wisdom and the most radiant beauty, which our dull faculties can comprehend only in their most primitive forms—this knowledge, this feeling, is at the center of true religiousness. In this sense, and in this sense only, I belong to the rank of devoutly religious men.

—Albert Einstein, as quoted in Philip Frank, *Einstein: His Life and Times* (1947)

Every system is perfectly designed to get the results it gets.

—W. Edwards Deming

Learning is not compulsory but neither is survival.

—W. Edwards Deming

Preface

American Football is not something I grew up with; it is an acquired taste developed in the last 20 years of frequenting and eventually living in North America. I was drawn into it by a friend who was very knowledgeable; he made me understand some of the intricacies of the game and spurred an interest that I cultivated over the years.

Football is a highly complex game that requires a truly systemic view of the organization; from the owner to the people that run the cafeteria, hundreds of individuals and variables have to be orchestrated to create something that is more than the sum of its (fast-moving) parts. A Football team is an ongoing network of projects with one, well-understood goal: Moving the Chains.

This is what successful organizations do: they have a plan and they execute on the plan. And when the going gets tough, to quote the iconic Bill Belichick, "they grind it out and they find a way to win." The inches they need are everywhere.

But in order to do so, organizations, in life and in football, need stability and focus: a well-laid out system and a leverage point they must exploit and subordinate to. Only in this way can they take the maximum out of the ingenuity, talent, and commitment of their people.

The goal of this book is to provide a conceptual framework and a set of guidelines for the development of an organizational design that can move the chains faster and replace the outdated, yet still prevailing, hierarchical/functional model.

This new design, which we call the "Network of Projects," is the offspring of a management paradigm that sees Quality of all work processes, people's active Involvement, and accelerated Flow of cash generation as the foundational elements for an effective and sustainable organization in this day and age.

The ever-growing level of complexity and interconnectedness of our times can be, at least partially, addressed by organizations with a well thought out use of digital technologies. It is imperative, though, to understand that digital technology requires a very profound rethinking of the way we work, and leaders cannot shy away from the responsibilities that come with this awareness.

Moving the Chains is primarily, yet not exclusively, aimed at decision makers. It has the ambition to engage the reader in a dialogue on what, ultimately, is in today's world the meaning of leadership; value chains grow exponentially in complexity; digitization imposes a speed on human activities never seen before in history; and a more and more decentralized, informed, and tech-savvy workforce demands a new covenant with their work.

Moving the Chains is not about a new management technique. It is about a too long overdue epistemological stance on how humans can meaningfully work together to accomplish complex endeavors. To do so, the author has leveraged the unparalleled contribution to the science of management provided by Dr. W. Edwards Deming and Dr. Eliyahu M. Goldratt, of blessed memory.

Their towering intellect and monumental body of knowledge provide the foundation for designing and guiding complex networks of value-added activities and paves the way for an entirely new approach to a New Economics based on sustainability and meaningfulness.

Acknowledgments

Moving the Chains builds upon 10 years of continuous interplay between "on the field" work and books, scientific papers, talks, podcasts, and blogs developed with my wife Dr. Angela Montgomery and Dr. Giovanni Siepe, my partners and lifetime comrades in the quest for a more evolved, meaningful, and overall Intelligent kind of Management. This book belongs to them just as much as it belongs to me.

In order to exemplify the concept of "Network of Projects" as a way of redesigning the organization as well as providing a useful tool for its adoption, Intelligent Management has leveraged the mathematical talent of Dr. Francesco Siepe who developed the sophisticated algorithm behind "Ess3ntial" and the wit and ingenuity of two of his best associates, Francesco Giugliano and Nicola Vastola. There aren't enough words to commend the relevance of their work for the dissemination of our message.

Getting to understand some of the intricacies connected with developing and implementing digital technologies was made possible by a constant collaboration and cooperation with our friends at Hyphen-Italia in Affi, Verona, Italy; Stefano Righetti and his talented team of "Lakeside Madmen" saw, many years ago, the need to conceive their products in a logic of flow and never surrendered to the difficulties of getting across to their clients a systemic view of the work of organizations. Stefano's chapter describes his personal journey with Digital and adds significantly to the clarity of the message this book tries to convey.

The association with Rik Willard and Dafne Ginn at Agentic in NYC has been invaluable to widen my horizon on the possibilities (and potential drawbacks) of Blockchain, perhaps the most intriguing and controversial of all the digital technologies, and helped me access a network of specialists that all over the world are testing the realm of its applicability. In the United States, I also want to thank two wonderful people, Patricia "PK" Keiran and Janet Granger, for their friendship and for sharing my professional crusade. Your smarts and inventiveness never cease to inspire me.

During the time of the writing of this book, I also completed the path toward citizenship in my country of residence, Canada. It has been a long and, at times, emotionally cumbersome, journey and I want to thank Seth Dalfen and his team in Montreal for helping me make this wonderful country home. I am very proud to be a "New Canadian."

To my oldest and dearest friends, who live miles away and yet are so present in my life with their expert counsel, care, and insight in all things connected with physical and psychological well-being; the gift of their love is invaluable to me: Dr. Luigi Capuano and Dr. Pasquale Cirillo, I want you to know that you mean the world to me.

The seemingly endless possibilities opened by Digital can only be fully and meaningfully exploited within a framework that is not only epistemological but also spiritual and ethical. I found this framework in the teachings and wisdom of Rabbi Menachem Mendel Schneerson, the Lubavitcher Rebbe of blessed memory; from the bottom of my heart, I want to thank my dearest friend Rabbi Chaim Miller, Lubavitcher Extraordinaire, for his constant and loving teachings (and for not losing his wonderful English accent even after many years in our beloved New York).

Last, and certainly not least, my mother Giulia and my "more than siblings", Giulia and Piero who never ceased to support me, spiritually and emotionally, in my journey of continuous discovery; I hope I make you proud.

Domenico Lepore, Victoria, BC, Canada, February 15, 2019
www.intelligentmanagement.ws
www.ess3ntial.com

CHAPTER 1

From Physical to Digital: Fundamental Questions for Radical New Answers

We now realize with special clarity, how much in error are those theorists who believe that theory comes inductively from experience.
—Albert Einstein, Physics and Reality, 1936

A theory can be proved by experiment but no path leads from experiment to the birth of a theory.
—Albert Einstein, from *Sunday Times*, 1976

This book is being written at the beginning of 2019. As I write, all the major English-speaking newspapers, magazines, TV channels, and blogs try to illustrate the catastrophic events that seem to be shaping the future of the western world: the inability of the European Union and North America to deal with the issue of mass migration, the blindness of governments toward looming environmental risks, the development of new and entirely artificial barriers to trade, the call for physical walls that should keep countries safer, the multiplication of unbridled ambitions to regain local sovereignty, changes in consolidated post-WWII alliances, meddling in elections, and so on.

In order to keep up with these events, an incessant flow of information is produced to provide every last detail in the evolution of situations; all good, but is this information capable of providing insight into what is likely to happen next? Is this tsunami of news helpful in helping us predict what the outcome of a situation is going to be?

On a much smaller yet far from irrelevant scale, this is what happens in the life of organizations: Management drowns in data and information.

These are by the way two *very* different categories—*information* is the result of the application of a thought process to the reading of *data*: a train timetable is data; the 5 pm from platform 3 is the information you seek when looking to get to Grand Central from Yonkers by 6 pm. While drowning in information and data, Management seems to be oblivious to Knowledge. Maybe it is useful to recall the difference: As Don Wheeler has said, "Information is random and miscellaneous; Knowledge is orderly, cumulative (and has a temporal spread)."

To be knowledgeable as leaders in the digital age requires understanding the problems raised by *complexity*, that is, a reality that is highly interconnected and interdependent. A great deal of management is, instead, "mechanistic." We are living in an age of "management crisis" because so many leaders are unaware of the appropriate knowledge to manage the complexity. This knowledge exists and this book aims to present it. Management knowledge can only come from solid theory; this knowledge advances thanks to the continuous feedback that takes place between the theory and the experience gained from its application on the field.

Knowledge, Theory, and Experience

Before I began working in the field of management, I was educated as a physicist. However, it is not necessary to be a scientist to appreciate that from Galileo Galilei and Newton onwards, all the things that we know (as opposed to those "that we think we know") and any meaningful advance in the human condition came from formulating a Theory and validating its realm of applicability. It is called the Scientific Method and it is high time for Management to fully embrace it.

We can start by understanding that Knowledge is built on Theory, a set of assumptions that allow prediction. A Theory has a realm of validity. This validity must be challenged by observation, and the boundaries of its applicability must be constantly revised.

In order for Knowledge to be useful, it needs Operational Definitions because they provide a way of putting communicable meaning into a concept, of translating a concept into a measurement of some sort.

Why does Management need Theory? Because Management must be rooted in prediction: without theory, the job of managers becomes a "whack-a-mole" exercise devoid of any ability to predict the outcome of their actions. Management also needs Theory because nothing can be learned from examples and experience without Theory; without it we would not be able to *interpret* the results of our observations. For this reason, studying case histories, as many Business Schools ask their students to do, makes little sense. And although thousands of examples do not make a Theory, *one example that contradicts a theory is sufficient to redesign the boundaries of a Theory's validity.* This is how science advances.

The kind of Knowledge that we need and that should inform leaders in Industry, Government, Health Care and Education, was put forth by Dr. W. Edwards Deming (American statistician and physicist) in his seminal book *The New Economics* and takes the name of the Theory of Profound Knowledge (TPK).

What it advocates is for management to commit to take a knowledge-based stance, to understand the "field of forces" that shapes the reality of an organization and to position events within the right framework. TPK moves management from the quicksand of empiricism (experience, opinion, examples) to the safe shore of epistemology (Knowledge).

There are four foundational elements that make up Deming's Theory. I have taken the intellectual liberty to (slightly) adapt Deming's elements in light of the last 25 years of on-the-field development:

1. Systems Theory (how the whole can be bigger than its parts)
2. Theory of Variation (that provides a rational foundation for understanding process behavior)
3. Theory of Knowledge (how we know what we know—Philosophy of mind, Epistemology, and Neuroscience operate/act according to a theory so as to have a reasonable conceptual handle on the outcome of our actions)
4. Psychology of the individual and the organization, the role that emotions play in human cognition and behavior (and massively impact process variation) as well as the collective psychology of the organization

These four elements are all *interdependent* and what emerges from understanding how these interconnections operate is nothing short of a new organizational and economic paradigm.

This new paradigm is based on cooperation, whole system optimization, a win–win mindset all along the value chains, and openness and transparency in every aspect of work and business interaction. It calls for an understanding of complexity and a radical overcoming of the silo mentality that still rules much of corporate life; it is firmly focused on designing, sourcing, producing, and distributing goods and services that improve people's lives; it rests on the assumption that humans are intrinsically motivated to do good, take pride in their work, and have an innate desire to learn and be part of something bigger than themselves.

This New Economics that Dr. Deming brings is one of sustainability. It is a radical departure from the Wall Street fantasies of deregulation and greed. The sheer inability to understand the consequences of deregulation and greed have propelled us into the neurological meltdown we are still experiencing in terms of unsustainable inequality.

Sustainability is predicated upon our understanding the laws that govern complexity—what happens when we begin to interact. The New Economics becomes, then, an economics of integration, where the network-like nature of our economies is understood at its most fundamental level.

The New Economics is based on well-studied and understood elements of Knowledge; sadly, these are still largely ignored in Business School curricula that are still mainly based on Finance and Cost Accounting principles and the mindset of local optima that they create. As Dr. Deming used to say, "Business Schools teach how to raid NOT how to lead a company."

So, why bother? Why this seemingly quixotic quest for "Profound Knowledge?"

The Digital Age

In the last 10–15 years, two major technological step-changes have taken place that have impacted drastically our reality: digitization and decentralization. Digitization is affecting (almost) every aspect of the human experience. Intimately connected with digitization, the way we work is becoming increasingly decentralized.

For most of the 1990s, a good portion of our daily interactions was *physical*: we would read papers, buy our clothes in shops, receive letters (with stamps!), use CDs and DVDs, go to meeting places with the goal of encountering other humans, even take pictures with "films," and pay with cash. There was a *physics* (mostly solid state) that would explain how things would work and a relatively well-tested psychology that would account for human interactions. Even computer programming languages had some level of connection with the physical circuits that would execute their commands.

The chain of events that would move an idea to its fruition followed a series of steps that were, in some way, under some level of our cognitive control. Even the most ethereal of business activities, Marketing, seemed to follow some "real life" cycle. Activities intimately connected with an (almost) entirely physical reality were aided by very precise structures: buildings, offices, organizational hierarchies, well-defined careers, and spans of individual control. With some exceptions, even the thought process guiding our actions was reassuringly "linear."

Today, we live most of our lives online and our cognitive experience, especially in millennials or younger, is dramatically influenced by it. The traditional workplace is being replaced by much more virtual and decentralized forms of collaboration. The mental covenant that binds us to the organizations we work for is changing and is more and more influenced by the idea of "personal branding" and icons and illustrations are rapidly replacing traditional reading materials in the learning process. The *network of networks* we are all part of, linguistically and otherwise, obeys mathematical laws that challenge our intuition and that we struggle to grasp. When so hard pressed by the need to make faster and much more complex choices, our brain just gives in and we succumb to a multiplicity of "cognitive tunnels."

We are not in Kansas anymore and we could certainly do with a yellow brick road. There is a growing number of beautifully labeled magic potions, all aimed at making us more Agile and Lean, impervious to the perils of VUCA, more adept to the inevitability of having to SCRUM, chained to ever-growing and decentralized Blocks, and so on.

Let me make a modest, old-fashioned proposal: let's try to understand what we are talking about.

> *The classical theorists resemble Euclidean geometers in a non-Euclidean world who, discovering that in experience straight lines apparently parallel often meet, rebuke the lines for not keeping straight—as the only remedy for the unfortunate collisions which are occurring. Yet, in truth, there is no remedy except to throw over the axiom of parallels and to work out a non-Euclidean geometry. Something similar is required today in economics.*
>
> —John Maynard Keynes

Digital technology is the offspring of a precise paradigm of togetherness; it is originated by the belief that conversations aimed at creating meaning through language cannot be hindered by filters that do not add value.

Digital technology is reshaping the way we cooperate through more meaningful interdependencies—the way we share information and the way we create possibilities for action. It is the natural consequence of the human drive toward better and more meaningful forms of interaction and communication. Its development was the inevitable, evolutionary outcome of the quest for understanding how our being together, in all its forms, can be enhanced.

The scientific foundation for digital technology can be found in the groundbreaking work of Shannon and Weaver on Information Theory; its philosophical roots are in the attempt to overcome the inherent limitation to communication of static devices. Simple (and not so simple) technologies like, for example, APIs are a testament (and an incipit) to this worldview: a new covenant in the way we can share and collaborate.

In order to honor such a covenant and allow it to give birth to the wealth of possibilities it foreshadows, deliberate effort is required from the institutions that should embrace it. Industry, Government, Education, Health Care, etc. must rise to the occasion and start rethinking themselves in light of these possibilities. This entails a fundamental shift in how we go about management: it requires both a new organizational design and a much more elevated form of organizational and individual consciousness.

Collaborative Work

Digital can (and will) be the trigger for the transformation of the current style of management that is embedded in, and epitomized by, the hierarchical, siloed organizational structure, into one of whole system optimization. The systems view of the organization that this book proposes *reshapes value chains and redesigns how interactions and conversations are possible.* It also calls for a complete shift in mindset and advocates an entirely new set of "coordinates" not unlike the ones in the foregoing quotation from Keynes. Such coordinates entail a completely different paradigm also in respect of the way we deal with our cognition processes. Digital technology propels and dramatically simplifies conversations and in this way it impresses on human cognition an unprecedented acceleration. It is one that is hard for many to cope with.

A blatant manifestation of the entirely new cognitive landscape that digital technology has brought about is the rapid growth of the decentralization of work. Despite all the bru-ha-ha around the alleged importance of a new kind of "coin," unearthed bit-by-bit from the crevices of computation, the real relevance of the technology that underpins it, Blockchain, is in the entirely new swathe of opportunities it creates for collaborative work.

Truly collaborative work cannot exist and cannot be developed within conventional frameworks such as existing siloed structures or behind the psycho-walls that fuel divisiveness. Decentralized, just like Billy Joel's New York, is a state of mind. Decentralized is a worldview that emerges as a result of the unprecedented need we have for communication. It underpins a paradigm of speed of flow through an entirely different set of interactions based on trust.

Said in a different way, digital technology is putting individuals and organizations alike under a hard-to-handle level of pressure to change, learn, and generate meaning through language. We need a new framework, a new system of coordinates and a compass to navigate the entirely different waters that the digital world has created.

This is precisely what a Theory provides. Theory, in any educated conversation, is not the opposite of Practice; it is what must guide any practice that aims at being sustainable over time.

A Theory to design and manage organizations in the digital age exists, and what follows in this book has the ambition to explain how to apply it successfully.

Summary of Chapter 1

- Leaders and managers are drowning in Information and Data when what they need is Knowledge.
- Without Theory, we cannot interpret information or predict outcomes of decisions and actions.
- W. Edwards Deming's Theory of Profound Knowledge provides the framework we need.
- There is a new paradigm for economic sustainability.
- Digital technology is ushering in a mindset based on value and collaboration.
- Our cognitive experience is shifting from physical and linear to a network of networks.
- We need a new set of coordinates and compass to navigate the digital world and its complexity.
- The pressure to change is unprecedented.
- A theory and method to design and operate organizations in the Digital Age exists and this book aims to explain how to apply it successfully.

CHAPTER 2

Mechanistic Thinking, Silos, and the New World of Complexity

The collaborative work that the Digital Age requires cannot exist and cannot be developed within conventional frameworks such as existing siloed structures. If silos keep organizations stuck, why do they exist at all? To understand this, we have to look at where mechanistic thinking comes from in the first place.

Sir Isaac Newton is arguably one of the greatest minds in human history. He developed the whole conceptual apparatus for the scientific revolution to happen; still today, from designing tables and chairs to sending a human being into space (and getting him/her back again), a large part of our existence obeys and can be understood in the light of the laws of nature he uncovered. Basically, anything that is not too small or not too fast is subject to Newton's laws.

The method of investigation he developed, the Scientific Method, has allowed fundamental discoveries in every aspect of the physical world: by breaking things down and understanding the pieces, we gain insight. We gain knowledge that dispels superstition, the offspring of ignorance. No amount of words would suffice to praise his genius and his contribution to mankind.

The influence of Newtonian thinking has been immense and, indeed, it has been the engine for the myriads of life-altering innovations that the industrial revolution spurred. In order to succeed, this "revolution" needed an infrastructure, a way of allowing people to make their efforts converge toward a common goal, what we call today "an organization."

Unsurprisingly (and unwittingly), organizations in their development followed the Newtonian approach: they broke down the whole into pieces to allow a better understanding of its functioning and, as we are

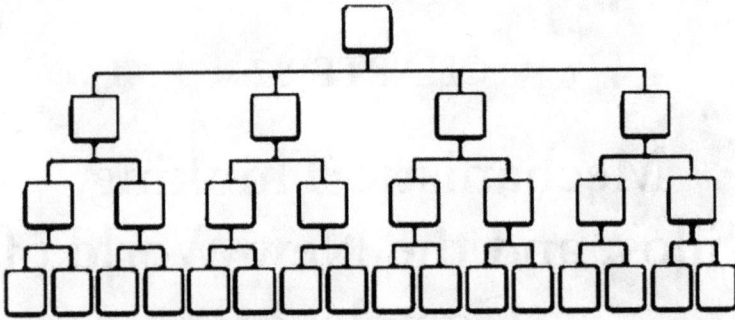

Figure 2.1 **A hierarchy**

talking industry and making money here, the way to control them. The Functional organization was born, as well as the Hierarchy that goes with it, represented in Figure 2.1.

What Is a Hierarchy?

Let's make a small digression.

Hierarchy is not a "bad thing"; it is an inherent part of any sustainable evolution and, neurologically, accounts for a robust set of synapses, the ones formed over several millennia by a large part of the human species. In fact, Hierarchy is what Jethro proposed to Moses in order to devise a mechanism to cope with the growing needs of legality that the unruly Israelites were creating.

> ...and you shall appoint over them [Israel] leaders over thousands, leaders over hundreds, leaders over fifties, and leaders over tens.
> And they shall judge the people at all times, and it shall be that any major matter they shall bring to you, and they themselves shall judge every minor matter, thereby making it easier for you, and they shall bear [the burden] with you.
> —Exodus, 18:21

Unfortunately, the biblical meaning of Hierarchy—levels of competencies—very rapidly regressed (as opposed to evolved) in orga-nizations into one of separation, epitomized by non-communicating silos and fueled by unintelligent, self-referential technology and ways

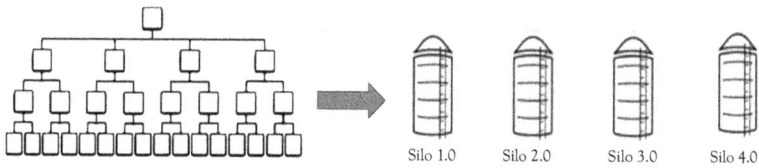

Figure 2.2 Hierarchies lead to silos

of accounting for performance. Still today, human setups such as Law Firms use horribly anachronistic metrics like "revenue per square foot" as a result of this lack of understanding (Figure 2.2).

Hierarchies are, instead, *a way of arranging competencies for a common goal*; this has become increasingly more obvious with the exponential increase in interactions that has characterized the last 20 years. Such a level of interactions has a name—Complexity—and has made a whole new set of properties "emerge."

This is where the Newtonian edifice shows some cracks; for Newton, the world was clockwork-like, a perfect mechanism of interacting, unchanging parts where everything was completely predictable in its evolution.

What we have come to understand scientifically in the last century is now very clearly manifesting itself through digital technology: we need radically different ways to allow people to collaborate *within* organizations and *among* them. We need a new organizational paradigm that can help us deal with the *emergent properties* that are the result of much more tightly knit interactions. We need to address what we have come to call the Dilemma of Complexity.

Understanding Complexity

We can address the Dilemma of Complexity by using a systemic Thinking Process from the Theory of Constraints.

The Conflict Cloud Thinking Process teaches us that a highly effective way to frame a complex situation is to think of it in terms of conflicting positions, legitimate needs that provoke those conflicting positions, and a common goal. Once we have framed a situation in this way, we can then surface all the assumptions (mental models) that keep us stuck in any given conflict or situation of blockage. When we have identified all these elements, we have a way to allow a win–win solution to emerge. This approach can be used at a variety of levels, from solving day-to-day problems to analyzing and solving highly complex issues.

Let's take managing organizations and complexity as an example. Here, we are going to look at the conflict of complexity, in other words, two possible and conflicting approaches to dealing with complexity.

The first position in the conflict is: *Manage complexity by breaking it up into its parts, or structures.* Why would we want to do that? What is the *need* we try to protect by adopting this position? We can verbalize that need as *understand the components.* The opposite, conflicting position is: *Manage complexity by focusing on the interactions and dynamics, or patterns.* Again, why would we want to do that? What is the *need* we try to protect by adopting this position? We can verbalize that need as *understand the interdependencies.* The common goal to both needs, the necessary conditions, is to *manage complexity.*

Now that we have pinned down the conflicting positions, we can start to surface all the assumptions that keep us stuck wondering which of these two positions is the best way ahead.

If the goal is to *manage complexity* and we assume that *an element of complexity is its components,* then that leads us to want to *break the complexity into its parts* to understand them better. On the other hand, if the goal is to *manage complexity* and we assume that *complexity is generated by interdependencies,* then we want to *focus on the interactions and dynamics, or patterns.*

How do we move forward out of this conflict? How can we find a solution that allows us to achieve the common goal, to manage complexity, and at the same time respect the legitimate needs to understand the components as well as the interdependencies? How can we do that without swinging like a pendulum between two opposite and conflicting positions?

This is where we see the power of the Conflict Cloud. We take the two conflicting positions and we surface the assumptions that keep us stuck. Why do we believe that we must *either* break the complexity into its parts *or* focus on the interactions and dynamics? It's because we make a series of assumptions, and if we can invalidate those assumptions (essentially mental models that do not have any value of truth), then we can find a way ahead.

We can verbalize the assumptions between the conflicting positions of "parts" versus "interactions" here as follows: (1) the whole is equal to the sum of its parts; (2) no new properties emerge from interactions among the parts; (3) interactions among the parts are always and only deterministic and linear (mechanistic view).

Now that we have verbalized those assumptions and they are "out in the open," we have cleared a path to find a solution that will allow us to lead and manage organizations in a way that is appropriate, adequate, and effective for today's complex reality. Figure 2.3 shows how we organize graphically a conflict cloud.

In order to "evaporate" this dilemma and forge ahead in redesigning more meaningful and effective organizations, we need to find a systemic solution that invalidates its underlying assumptions while respecting the needs that have originated the dilemma. In the Theory of Constraints, we call such a systemic solution an "injection." (The technical definition of an "injection" in TOC is a statement that invalidates the assumptions between the conflicting positions of the cloud while respecting both needs.)

To generate such an injection, some elements of Knowledge are needed and they come from the monumental body of work developed, separately, by Dr. W. Edwards Deming (1900—1993) and Dr. Eliyahu Goldratt (1947—2011). In the last 20 years, my effort has been to integrate and evolve the work of Deming and Goldratt to make it suitable for a complete overhaul of the prevailing, silo-based organizational design and cost-driven management style. I published the various stages of development and implementations of this integration of Deming and Goldratt first with Oded Cohen in the book *Deming and Goldratt: The Decalogue* (1999) and later in *Sechel: Logic, Language and Tools to Manage Any Organization as a Network* (2011), and more recently with Giovanni Siepe and Angela Montgomery in a chapter for Springer called "Managing Complexity in Organizations Through a Systemic Network of Projects" (2015) and our book *Quality, Involvement, Flow: The Systemic Organization* (2016). I am, indeed, forever indebted to the many companies and to their leaders and teams that over the last two decades adopted these principles in their organizations.

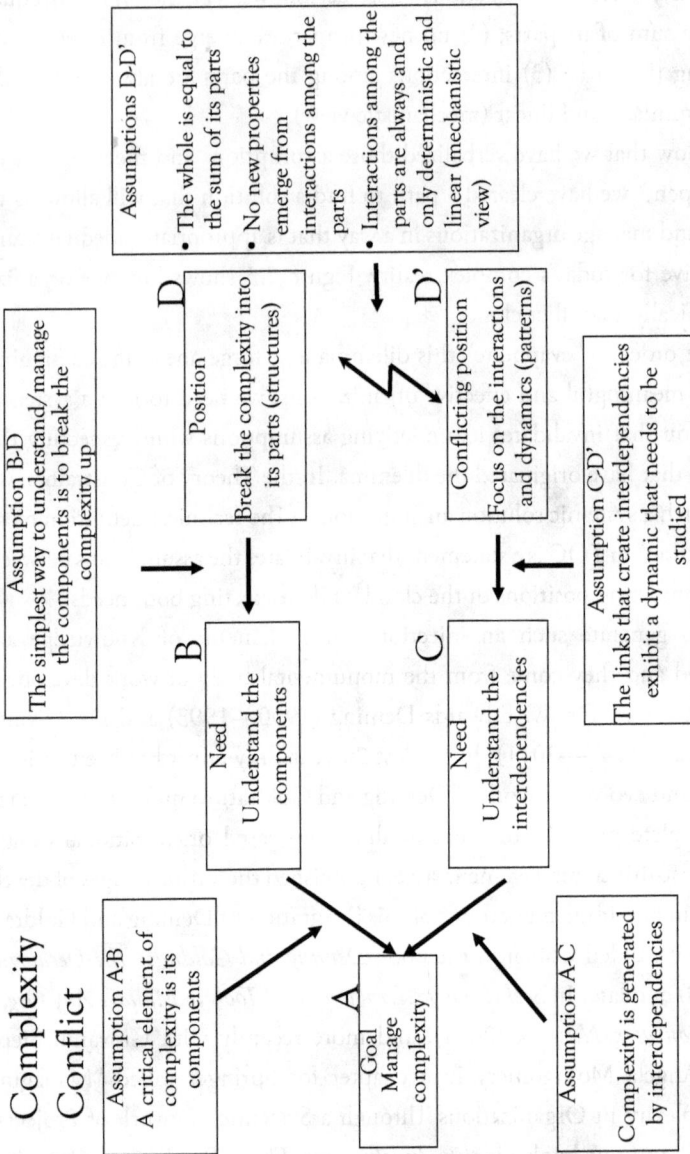

Complexity Conflict

Assumption A-B
A critical element of complexity is its components

A
Goal
Manage complexity

Assumption A-C
Complexity is generated by interdependencies

B
Need
Understand the components

C
Need
Understand the interdependencies

Assumption B-D
The simplest way to understand/manage the components is to break the complexity up

D
Position
Break the complexity into its parts (structures)

D'
Conflicting position
Focus on the interactions and dynamics (patterns)

Assumption C-D'
The links that create interdependencies exhibit a dynamic that needs to be studied

Assumptions D-D'
• The whole is equal to the sum of its parts
• No new properties emerge from interactions among the parts
• Interactions among the parts are always and only deterministic and linear (mechanistic view)

Figure 2.3 The complexity conflict

In the aforesaid publications, you can find a comprehensive account of this scientific, professional, and ultimately, cognitive journey. What follows in the ensuing chapters is a short summary for the purposes of this book.

Summary of Chapter 2

- Everything that is not too small or too fast is subject to Newton's laws.
- Newton envisaged a universe that was mechanical and where components were separate.
- This mechanical worldview underpins organizations envisaged as vertical hierarchies.
- Silos are the result of a lack of understanding of how to govern interactions where complexity exists.
- Complexity is characterized by a large number of interdependencies that cannot be cut into separate components.
- Complexity calls for a new understanding of how to govern interactions and a new organizational design that can shift away from a silo-based model.
- The Knowledge provided by Dr. W. Edwards Deming (Theory of Profound Knowledge) and Dr. Eliyahu Goldratt (Theory of Constraints) provides the basis for a new understanding of how to design and manage organizations for complexity.

CHAPTER 3

Overcoming the Hierarchical/Functional Model with 10 Transformational Steps

In Chapter 1, I tried to explain why we need a Theory: without it, we would not know how to evaluate the outcome of what we do; we would not have any framework within which to gauge our actions, any backcloth against which to assess our decisions, or any guideline to drive our efforts toward any chosen goal.

A Theory is then needed when the radical changes brought about by digitization are foreshadowing a new organizational paradigm. It is one we can no longer afford to forego.

Digital technology is accelerating the ever-present quest that sustainably successful organizations must pursue: Quality of processes achieved through active Involvement of people that maximize the Flow of products, services, information, and money. Quality, Involvement, Flow.

The elements of the Theory we need must then be connected with how to achieve Quality, Involvement, and Flow and, for the purposes of this book, how they can help with the design of an organization fit for Complexity.

Some visuals can help.

Dr. Deming, long before anybody else, understood that organizations are systems, networks of components that work together toward a common goal. In order to achieve this in practice, such components must operate in a state of statistical predictability; otherwise chaos will ensue. Statistical Predictability is the result of processes, methods, and technologies operated by people sharing a precise epistemological framework, who are intrinsically motivated, hence cognitively involved in achieving a goal that betters their lives and the world around them.

(This is my quick take on the overarching vision for Quality that Dr. Deming put forth and, of course, I take full responsibility for what I write.)

Such a system, depicted in Figure 3.1, was first designed for the benefit of Japanese industrialists in 1952, and it was fueled over the decades by a continuously growing body of knowledge, eventually formalized in two pillars of management theory, Deming's *Out of the Crisis* and *The New Economics*.

The arrows represent the systems' components (processes and projects the company is made up of) and in the circles I have highlighted its main features: focus on the client, feedback loops, emphasis on interdependencies.

Deming's "Production viewed as a system" was the starting point for the Quality movement and ushers in those elements of integration, collaboration, and transparency that are the hallmark of digital technologies.

Dr. Goldratt, a physicist like Deming, looked at how to emphasize and capitalize on the systemic nature of the work of organizations from a different angle. Any organizational system, he argued, can be designed so as to have only one element (or very, very few) that determines the pace at which it pursues its goal. Such an element, strategically chosen, i.e., capable of offering the highest value, becomes the leverage point that maximizes what the whole system can produce. He called it the "constraint."

In order to maximize the performance of the constraint (hence, the overall performance of the system):

(a) The constraint must be rationally *exploited*, meaning it must work constantly and on the most suitable mix of "products."

(b) The constraint must be fully *subordinated to*—in other words every other component in the system must be designed and operated so as to enhance the performance of the constraint.

(c) A protection mechanism must be put in place to prevent disruptions (mostly due to statistical unpredictability of processes) to the constraint. It is called a "Buffer."

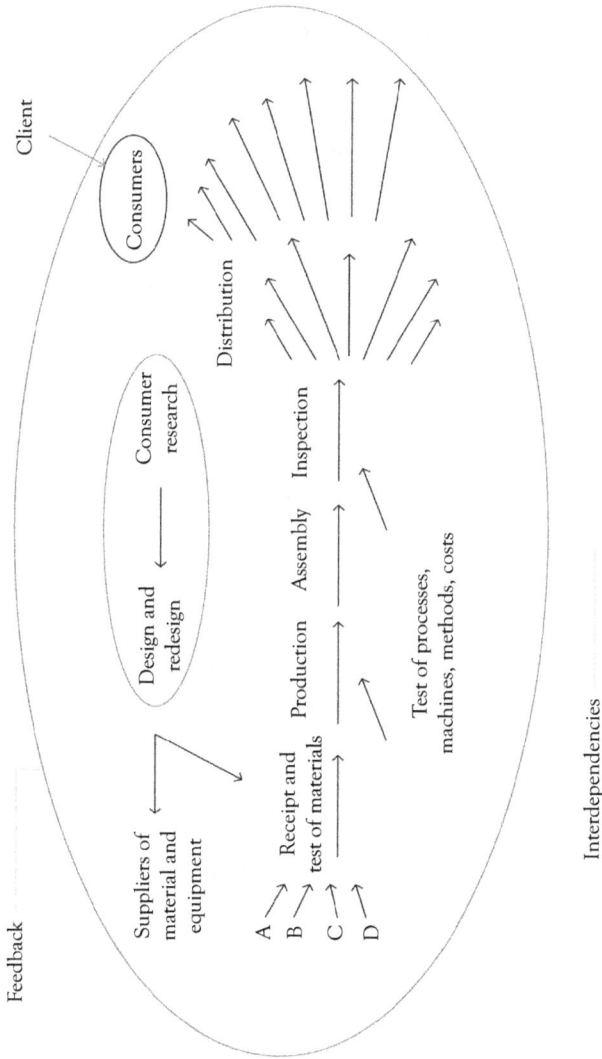

Figure 3.1 The organization as a system, based on Deming's original 1952 "Production Viewed as a System"

Around these deceptively simple concepts, Dr. Goldratt built a wealth of practical applications; more importantly, he developed a comprehensive theory, the Theory of Constraints (TOC), to illustrate all the aspects connected with designing, managing, and evolving a constraint-based organizational system.

Deming and Goldratt grew up in different countries, had different cultural heritages, belonged to different generations, and so was the language they used to illustrate their views and findings. I venture to say that they had radically different personalities, just like their followers and comrades.

Integrating Deming and the Theory of Constraints

Why did Oded Cohen, a leading figure in the TOC world, and I feel the need for a cohesive and rigorous integration of Deming and Goldratt's message? What is the purpose of the new resulting message that we called *The Decalogue* (meaning "10 steps")? What emerges from the integration of Deming and TOC?

For me, at the time, the main drive was scientific: I wanted to see the thinking of these two giants finally unified and expressed in a language that would give justice to their common lifetime goal of providing a more meaningful, intelligent, evolved role for management and leadership. The outcome of this effort, I thought, could be a step ahead in the human quest for better reasoning.

The Decalogue, in its initial verbalization (1999), achieves the goal of laying out many of the prerequisites for sustainable wealth creation. Let's say that it identifies "the pieces" of the puzzle, but it does not put them together completely. More work was needed, but I am grateful to both Oded and our publisher at North River Press, Larry Gadd, for taking the chance. Today, I stand behind the Decalogue, as it has proven to be scientifically and methodologically very solid.

The questions in front of me were the following: Why have so (relatively) few companies embraced Deming or Goldratt (let alone the Decalogue)? What was the missing piece in their hugely complex body of knowledge? What stands in the way of its adoption?

While we progressed with perfecting methods to facilitate the understanding of the Decalogue, my team and I, working on both sides of the "pond," realized that any effort to promote the cognitive leap necessary to embrace the Decalogue would shipwreck against the prevailing organizational model: the Functional Hierarchy and the Silo mentality that it entailed. Before we look at that in more detail, we need to go back to the Complexity conflict.

Back to the Complexity Conflict

We use a conflict cloud to make a robust, cause–effect analysis of any situation in which we are stuck. When used in concert with the other Thinking Processes from the Theory of Constraints, the conflict cloud can help us generate powerful solutions that capitalize on our intuition, develop our understanding through analysis, and lead us to design a set of consistent actions that we can execute. The conflict cloud is a Thinking Process that everyone needs to learn. Let's look again at the complexity conflict.

What are the fundamental assumptions that underpin this conflict (depicted in Figure 3.2)?

- The whole is equal to the sum of its parts.
- No new properties emerge from interactions among the parts.
- Interactions among the parts are always and only deterministic and linear (mechanistic view).

So, if we want to escape this conflict, if we want to open up to a new way of designing organizations that overcomes the alleged duality of Local versus Global and of Parts versus Whole and that replaces the outdated silos with something more in line with the evolving needs of work, but at the same time can be controlled, we need a new image and a protocol to sustain it.

My team and I began to imagine a way to visually represent the kind of organizational system that the Decalogue would support. The result was published in our book *Sechel: Logic, Language and Tools to Manage Any Organization as a Network*, in 2011.

The organization design we developed was a breakthrough in terms of how to manage organizations using the Knowledge from both Deming and the Theory of Constraints. We were assisted in developing this

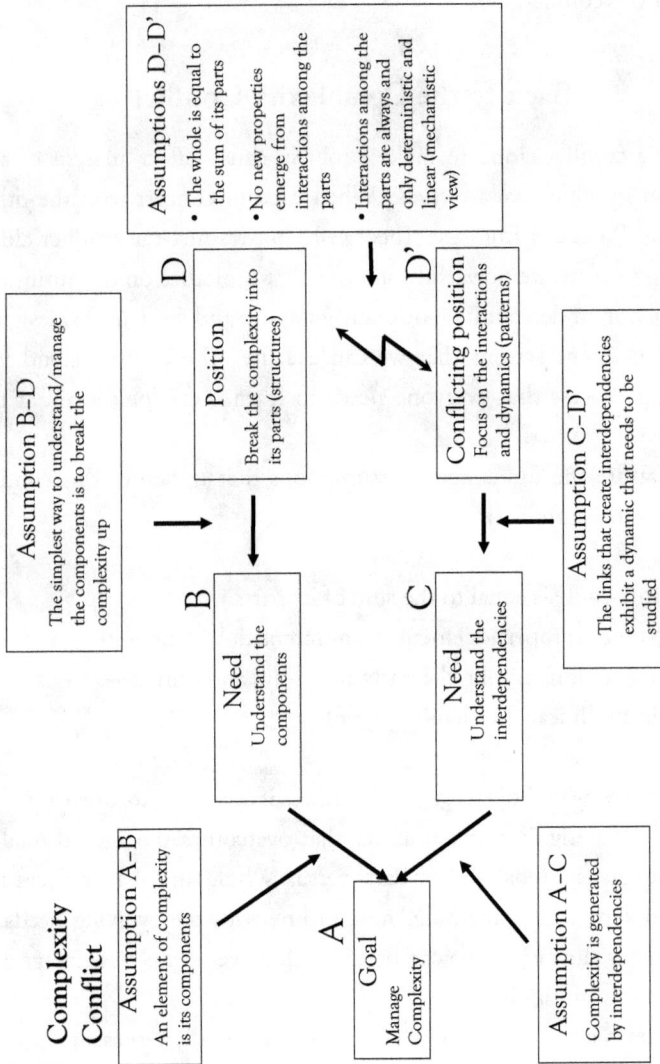

Complexity Conflict

Assumption A–B
An element of complexity is its components

A
Goal
Manage Complexity

Assumption A–C
Complexity is generated by interdependencies

B
Need
Understand the components

C
Need
Understand the interdependencies

Assumption B–D
The simplest way to understand/manage the components is to break the complexity up

Assumption C–D'
The links that create interdependencies exhibit a dynamic that needs to be studied

D
Position
Break the complexity into its parts (structures)

D'
Conflicting position
Focus on the interactions and dynamics (patterns)

Assumptions D–D'
• The whole is equal to the sum of its parts
• No new properties emerge from interactions among the parts
• Interactions among the parts are always and only deterministic and linear (mechanistic view)

Figure 3.2 The complexity conflict

breakthrough by following the Thinking Process of the conflict cloud. Our new organizational design became a system, as depicted by Deming in 1952, but where the interdependencies are designed around a strategically chosen constraint, for example, Production, as in our illustration. This constraint is protected by a buffer whose fluctuations are statistically understood. We called the visual depiction of this organizational design "The Systemic Organization Cartoon," illustrated in Figure 3.3.

Let's summarize: if we want to overcome the inherent limitations originated by a Newtonian worldview, we need to embrace the systemic elements of knowledge provided by Deming and TOC and we need to create a suitable organizational framework that allows this knowledge to be applied successfully.

The Systemic Organization Cartoon represents a *visual* injection (systemic solution) to the conflict of Complexity; this conflict is completely generic. Generic does not mean "overgeneralized." It means that *its validity is so strong that it can be tailored to different contexts.* Finding the appropriate verbalization is key to surfacing the blocking assumptions that keep us stuck in the conflict. (For any readers passionate about physics, as the Decalogue methodology was developed also by a physicist, we have added to the appendix a *divertissement* applied to the duality wave-particle found in quantum mechanics.)

For instance, if we want to tailor the Complexity conflict more specifically to the context of organizations, it can be usefully re-verbalized as Hierarchy versus *No* hierarchy.

What is the prevailing organizational structure and what is wrong with it? The conflict is a blatant one. On the one hand:

A hierarchy fails to acknowledge three critical aspects of the life of a successful company: interdependencies, feedback cycle, and the customer. For these reasons, it is not suitable for sustaining a continuous improvement effort.

On the other hand:

A hierarchy seems to cater for accountability and provides a sense of control.

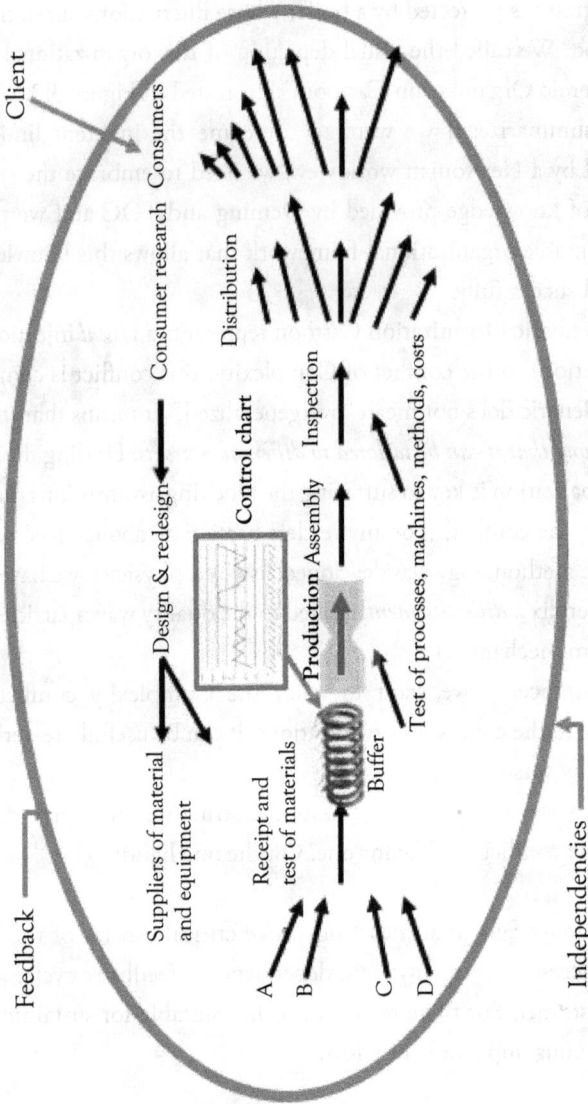

Figure 3.3 The systemic organization cartoon

The conflict rests, then, on the idea of *control* and how this idea is translated into a consistent, and consistently measured, organizational system.

Let's reorganize these thoughts using the Conflict Cloud Thinking Process. It is clear that the hierarchical model is inadequate and prevents organizations from unleashing their true potential. The traditional model for control is a hierarchical/functional structure (Figure 3.4).

The reasons why a hierarchical structure exists are the assumptions between B and D (Figure 3.5).

Increasing our capacity to listen to the customer so we can satisfy the needs of the market leads us to NOT adopt a hierarchical structure (Figure 3.6).

Figure 3.7 shows the pieces of the conflict we have looked at put together with the assumptions.

The two positions are in conflict because we believe the assumptions in the box on the far right in Figure 3.8.

This verbalization of the assumptions makes evident why the Systemic Organization Cartoon is an injection completely consistent with the teachings of Deming and Goldratt:

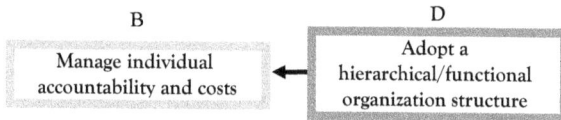

Figure 3.4 B and D in the hierarchy conflict

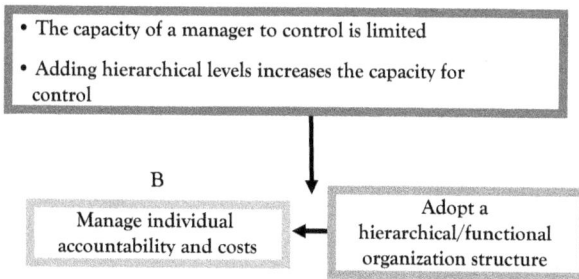

Figure 3.5 The assumptions between B and D

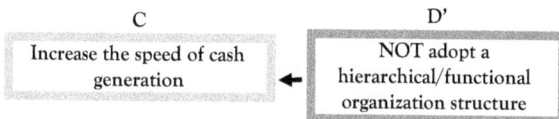

Figure 3.6 C and D' in the Hierarchy Conflict

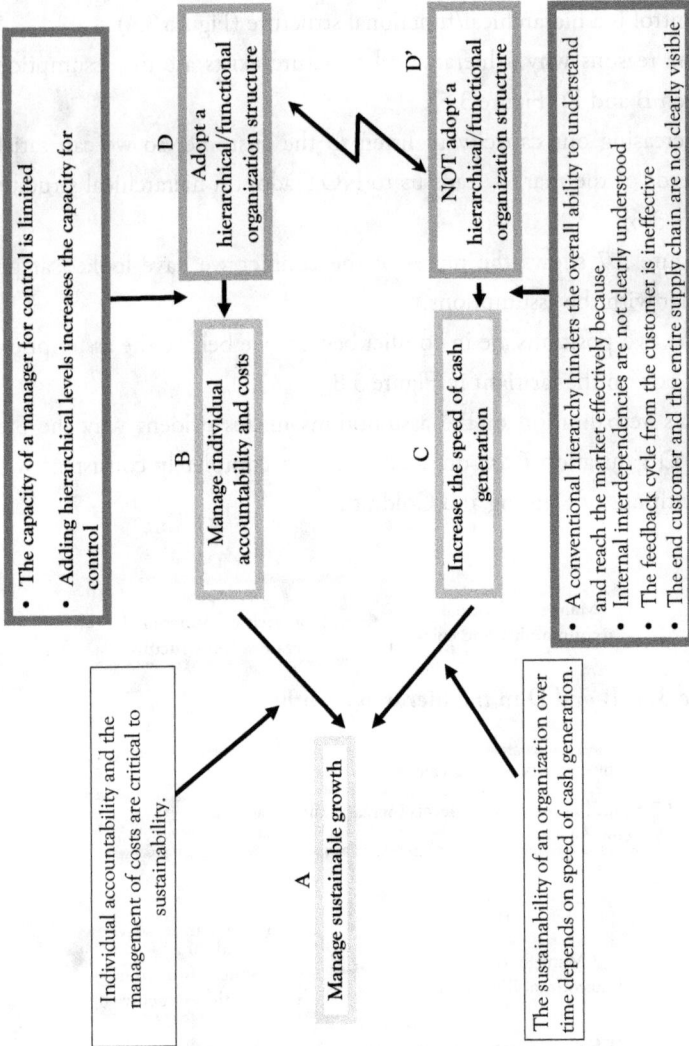

Figure 3.7 The Hierarchy Conflict with assumptions

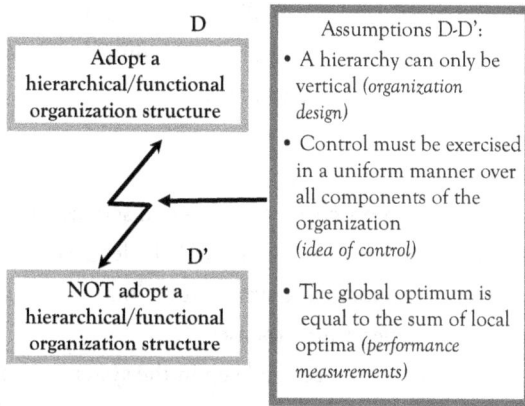

Figure 3.8 The assumptions between D and D' in the Hierarchy Conflict

1. Control is exerted by understanding statistical fluctuation in the buffer.
2. Design is Systemic, customer focused, and based on accelerated flow through tight collaboration among different competencies.
3. Global and Local optima are reconciled by subordinating the whole system to the constraint, hence avoiding the fallacies of cost allocation, functional budgeting, individual performance appraisal, etc.

The Systemic Organization Cartoon is the "injection" (systemic solution) to the conflict. What transforms this injection into reality is an *operational plan* that gives life to the Cartoon. This is what the Decalogue does.

The 10 Steps of the Decalogue

What follows is a brief explanation of the 10 Steps of the Decalogue.

Step 1: Establishing the goal of the system, the units of measurements, and the operational measurement
Without a goal, there is no system; and without clarity on what to measure in the system and how to measure it, talking about a goal becomes lip service. GAAP accounting utilized to support managerial decisions is the enemy number one of productivity. EBIT, EBITDA, EPS, and any form

of GAAP-derived measurements totally miss the point of what a company should strive for. If the goal of a company is connected in any way with making money, then all we need to know is:

- What comes in (Sales);
- What goes out to purchase materials and services that go into the products we sell (TVC, Totally Variable Costs);
- What we need to make the system function (fixed costs + investments), Operating Expenses (*OE*);
- The inventory (*I*) we need to keep in the system to ensure that we always have enough "material" to produce and ship.

These basic variables are connected in the following way:

Sales minus TVC = Throughput (T) *T* minus *OE* = Net Profit; *T* minus *OE* minus *I* = Cash Profit, the physical money we see in the bank account before tax. Indeed, from year to year, *I* becomes *Delta I*.

Throughput is overwhelmingly more important than Inventory and *OE* because it can potentially grow far more than *OE*, and *I* can be reduced only so much. Sadly, the whole GAAP effort revolves around "understanding *OE*" with devastating effects on decision making. Let us say this clearly: The industrial world is where real wealth can be created, and industry needs to learn how to measure its performances based on *T*, *I*, and *OE*. Banks, stock market, financial institutions, and the guild of accountants *must* understand that their job is to support true wealth creation by fostering in industry the pursuit of these measurements instead of thrusting upon them anything different.

Over 30 years ago, Dr. Goldratt explained these simple concepts, and all the financial and industrial catastrophes we have experienced in the last 25 years are, directly or indirectly, the result of not having understood them. Throughput is the most powerful way to link the industrial and the financial worlds, and the accounting that goes with it provides a whole new and meaningful scope to the endeavors of the accounting profession.

It is also critically important to measure how the system performs in its effort to deliver to customers. We can have a pretty good handle on it by measuring the on-time delivery and assigning a dollar value to any delay; we call it Throughput Dollar Day (*T$D*). The longer the delay, the higher the *T$D*. Similarly, we want to know how much cash we keep trapped in Inventory to achieve an optimal, ideally zero, *T$D*, and we call it Inventory Dollar Day (*I$D*).

Step 2: Understand the system (draw the interdependencies)

If we do not know who does what, what the inputs and outputs are, and how everybody's work is connected, then we are not managing. As we have mentioned, Dr. Deming declared that "Business schools teach you how to raid a company, not how to manage it." It is disconcerting to discover how little we know about our system until we have a clear picture of how our interdependencies are laid out and how neglected by top management this issue is. Through mapping out all the main processes of an organization, Step Two provides the foundational elements of understanding that will enable the building of a truly effective Quality System.

Step 3: Make the system stable (understand variation and its impact on the network)

Dr. Deming used to say that if he had to reduce his message to Management to just a few words, he would say that their job is all about *reducing variation*. Dr. Deming's unrivaled contribution to the science of management comes from having understood the importance (and all the implications) of a body of statistical studies developed by Dr. Walter Shewhart of Bell laboratories in the 1920s. Shewhart found out that any process is affected by variation, which is enemy number one of Quality and reliability; however, this variation can be attributed to either common causes or special ones. Distinguishing "noise" from "signal" was then critical to devising actions aimed at managing this variation. Dr. Shewhart developed an important part of the Theory of Variation known as Statistical Process Control (SPC) and a very useful mechanism for measuring variation called a Control Chart (also known as Process Behavior Chart). His work was foundational for the improvement of productivity, first at Bell and then in a myriad of organizations countrywide, and certainly served as a springboard for the gigantic work of Dr. Deming.

Dr. Deming realized that, in order to manage the variation associated with a process, people make two kinds of errors:

1. They attribute variation to a special cause when it is instead due to a common cause.
2. They attribute variation to a common cause when it is instead due to a special cause.

The ramifications of these errors are endless and still today plague the way companies make decisions; Statistical Process Control (SPC), the main body of knowledge from which the Theory of Profound Knowledge has evolved, is largely ignored at Top Management and Corporate level. SPC is neither a purely mathematical tool nor a conventional financial management tool. The process behavior charts mirror the outcome of our managerial decisions, often taken with some kind of local optima in mind. The image they portray is not the reassuringly deterministic one that accountants and financial people are accustomed to; on the contrary, what these charts display are predictable or unpredictable ranges of oscillation. These oscillations very often reflect, mercilessly, the conflicting confusion that dictates our choices, and the course of action that their interpretation calls for flies in the face of "conventional wisdom."

Understanding SPC, let alone using it properly and accurately, requires a paradigm shift in the way we look at data and make sense of them for business decisions. From a mathematical standpoint, process charts are based on an average dispersion statistics and the approach they use is the 3-sigma one for the calculation of limits. What has always generated confusion about SPC charts is that, although connected with probability theory, they do not work *because of* it. The essence of the charts is in their predictive role and in the possibility that they provide to build an epistemological approach to management based on prediction.

Control charts capture the most fundamental feature of the work of individuals and their interaction within an organization, the variation associated with processes. In building a systemic organization based on the Decalogue, SPC has a central role.

Step 4: Build the system around the constraint (subordinate the organization to the constraint)

The new kind of organization that is based on managing variation and constraints is a network of interdependent processes with one common goal where we have achieved a good level of statistical predictability. It can be successfully managed, but the question is, how? Dr. Goldratt's main contribution to the Theory of Management has been to point out that any system is limited toward its goal by very few elements, the constraints. If we identify them, we can manage them following the steps of focusing that he developed. The Decalogue, leveraging the intrinsic stability of a Deming-based system, suggests that the constraint can be "chosen" (one constraint) instead of being identified. In other words, we can always decide which constraint it is strategically more convenient to focus on and build the system accordingly. However, we can do it *only* because we have already built a system made of low variation processes; this is why we can safely design our company around a strategically chosen constraint. Instead of cycling the five focusing steps of TOC, namely, (1) identify the constraint, (2) exploit the constraint, (3) subordinate to the constraint, (4) elevate the constraint, and, if the constraint has moved, (5) go back to step (1), we can make the system grow by appropriately choosing the constraint and sizing the capacity of all the feeding/subordinating processes coherently. Again, this is possible only because the variation in the system is low.

Step 5: Manage the constraint (protect and control the system through Buffer Management)

The performance of this system is ensured by its predictability but we need a mechanism to protect it and control it. This is provided by the buffer and by its management. What is a buffer? Individual processes exhibit variation; two or more together do too, let's call it covariance. The effect of covariance is a cumulated variation that can result in any sort of combination of these variances. Regardless of how little individual variation the processes of the system have, we do need a mechanism to protect the most critical part of our organization, the constraint. A buffer is a quantity of *time* that we position in front of the constraint to protect it from the cumulative variation that the system generates. Simply put, in synchronizing the processes that deliver the output of our organization, we ensure that what has to be worked on by the constraint gets in front of it "one buffer time ahead."

Is there a precise and unequivocal recipe to size the buffer appropriately? No, and it doesn't matter. If you understand control charts, the sizing is fairly obvious. The real importance of the buffer is not in the protection from disruption, certainly not an irrelevant issue, but in the possibility to exert control over the functioning of the whole organization: If our processes are all predictable, then we can truly use the buffer as a mechanism to gather succinct, effective, and comprehensive information about the "state of synchronization" of our company. Indeed, if we monitor the buffer with the use of a control chart, then the control becomes real insight, the goal of management.

The management of the buffer entails a Copernican shift in the way we mean control because it prompts decision makers to rely on understanding and knowledge rather than on hunches; it forces them into leveraging arguably esoteric statistical studies instead of salt of the earth accounting; it constrains the unbridled vibrancy of managers into the straightjacket of rational thinking. As a result of those considerations, over the decades, many of the repeated attempts to introduce buffer management to Top Management have failed.

Step 6: Reduce variation of the constraint(s) and the main processes
Step Six is obviously connected to Step Five but less obviously to Step Seven. Clearly, we do understand the impact that variation has on our system and the need to reduce it but when push comes to shove, we are not prepared to continue to work on variability reduction. Why not? The answer is in our ability and desire to understand the purpose of system management.

The culturally disappointing translation of Deming's Philosophy into a plethora of "Kaizen-like" management techniques has transformed it from a vision of the world based on innovation and wealth creation into an efficiency game. If, on top of this, we continue to view our company in "functional" terms, then reducing variation simply means reducing costs. Of course, no function would ever easily surrender to that because it would imply "cutting the budget"; hence any serious attempt to reduce variation is nipped in the bud. A relentless effort toward continuous reduction in variation can only stem from a *systemic* vision of our company and the understanding that only this reduction would provide the insight needed for triggering real jumps in performance. The way to link a relentless, focused, and companywide variation reduction crusade to financial performance is through the adoption of a suitable organizational structure.

Step 7: Create a suitable management/organizational structure

At the time of publication of the book *Deming and Goldratt: The Decalogue* (1999), Step Seven was not clearly and comprehensively elucidated upon.

It was clear that, without a suitable structure, the realistic possibility to sell all the capacity of the constraint would be hindered by local optima considerations. In other words, the design of a suitable structure was a prerequisite for enabling the true expansion of the system. Today it is much clearer that the natural way to see the work of an organization is in terms of process and projects. In the years that followed, further research and application led to the development of the *Network of Projects* organizational design as a means to improve and optimize the performance of the whole system.

Step 8: Eliminate the external constraint (sell all the capacity the system has available)

When we design a system that caters for a high degree of process predictability and synchronization, where control and protection are ensured by buffers and where all the policies, behavioral, and measurement "constraints" are dealt with by an appropriate organizational structure, we do so to maximize sales. The most important part of the chain is the customer, and any company should always be designed to ever improve its ability to satisfy its customers' verbalized and hidden needs. The Decalogue, if understood and embedded in the appropriate structure, should very quickly reveal capacity that is not currently being sold.

Another way of looking at this issue is the following. Let's say that, day one, the rate of sales of a company starting its Decalogue journey was such that some shipments were missed and constant fire-fighting would create friction between production and sales. The Decalogue would call for a disciplined process mapping effort aimed at understanding process variability and the choice and management of a suitable constraint as well as the devising of a coherent measurement system. Moreover, in order for this level of synchronization not to be hindered by the local optima inclination that functional organizations invariably undergo, we would design an appropriate, coherent organizational structure. Almost invariably, the constraint would shift outside, become an "external constraint": our capacity, what we can realistically design, manufacture, and ship, would become greater than what we were currently capable of selling. At this point, it would be blatantly obvious that our real understanding of the market is woefully limited and we, in truth, do not know how to sell. Goldratt developed a powerful and detailed Thinking Process approach to managing the external constraint. This is a very critical point in the pattern of a successful Decalogue implementation. Why? When left to behave in a traditional local optima way, salespeople can singlehandedly jeopardize any systemic endeavor unless we integrate them organically into the way the company operates.

Step 9: Where possible, bring the constraint inside the organization and fix it there

The Decalogue approach to management is based on process stability; indeed the most critically important part of the system is the constraint. Hence, we want to ensure maximum predictability, especially on the constraint. Clearly, when the constraint is external such predictability is more difficult to achieve. This is the reason why, whenever possible, we want to manage an internal constraint. Moreover, this is also the easiest way to make the system grow without stirring chaotic company dynamics.

The need for constraint reliability is so strong that even when organizations have a virtually unlimited internal capacity, like supermarkets, we should always elect to appoint an internal constraint and subordinate the whole organization to it. The growth of the system would then happen through a systematic, orderly, and relentless exploitation of the capacity of the constraint. When such a capacity is not sufficient to meet market demand, we would first increase the appropriate non-constraint areas to make them capable of subordinating to the constraint and only then would we elevate (increase the capacity of) the constraint. Once again, the name of the game is process predictability.

Step 10: Create a continuous learning program

The possibility for a Decalogue-based management system to produce results over time rests on the ability that the organization has to continually learn what is needed to constantly improve its performances.

Learning does not happen in a vacuum and cannot be based solely on individual desire. Learning and personal development must become part of the way the organization functions, and the change associated with it must become a way of life for the company. Learning cannot be "installed," nor can it be forced on people. It must be a personal choice, but also an integral part of the way the company has structured itself to conduct business. Learning and the self-development that comes with it must be promoted companywide and from the Top Management, but must come from a designated and empowered source. Over the years, we have come to call it a Center for Learning.

The Decalogue is founded on the principle of continuous improvement. Not only does it employ the Plan, Do, Study, Act continuous improvement cycle designed by Deming, but the entire 10 steps embody that cycle pattern in the way they are carried out. This can be seen clearly when we map out the 10 steps of the Decalogue onto the PDSA cycle itself (Figure 3.9).

Summary of Chapter 3

- In order to embrace and make the most of the changes that digital technology is bringing, companies need to focus on improving Quality, Involvement, and Flow.
- Organizations are *systems*, networks of components that work together toward a common goal.
- The key focus areas for managing a company as a system are managing variation and managing a strategically chosen constraint.
- If we look at the conflict of Hierarchy versus No hierarchy, we see that the 10 transformational steps of the Decalogue provide a valid solution to shift away from silos and toward an organization as one whole, synchronized system. The Ten Steps are:

1. Plan:
Establish the goal of the system,
the units of measurements, and the operating measurements(1).
Understand the system–map the interdependencies (2)
Build the system around the constraint (4);

2. Do:
Make the System stable (3)
Manage the constraint -Buffer Management (5)
Createa suitable governing structure (Network of Projects) (7);

3. Study:
Reduce variation at (of) the constraint and the main processes (6)

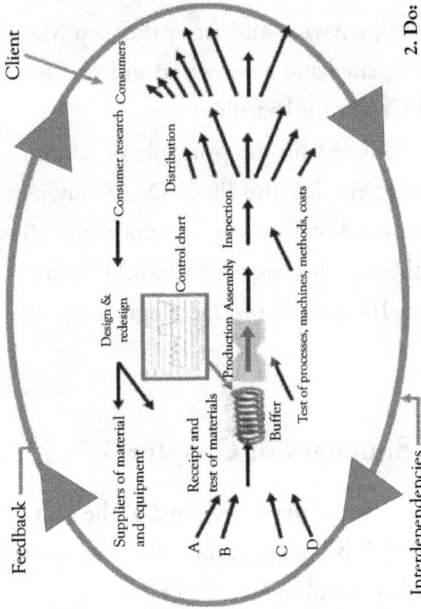

4. Act:
Eliminate the "external constraint"—sell all the capacity the system has available (8)
Where possible, bring the constraint inside the organization and fix it there (9)
Create a program of continuous learning (10)

Client

Consumer research Consumers

Distribution

Control chart

Design & redesign

Inspection

Production Assembly

Test of processes, machines, methods, costs

Receipt and test of materials

Buffer

Suppliers of material and equipment

A
B
C
D

Feedback

Interdependencies

Figure 3.9 Steps of the Decalogue mapped onto the PDSA cycle

1. Establish the goal of the System, units of measurement, and operational measurement
2. Understand the system (map the interdependencies)
3. Make the system stable (predictable)
4. Build the system around the constraint
5. Manage the constraint - Buffer Management
6. Reduce variation at (of) the constraint and the main processes
7. *Create a suitable management/organizational structure*
8. Eliminate the "external constraint" – sell all the capacity the system has available
9. Where possible, bring the constraint inside the organization and fix it there
10. Create a program of continuous learning

CHAPTER 4

Cooperation, Interaction, and Networks: A New Awareness

We are becoming increasingly aware of the need for collaboration and cooperation. Techniques such as Agile and DevOps require it. Collaboration as a principle is not yet mainstream for management and organizations, but the more complexity becomes the backdrop and context of what we do and experience, the more we need to find up-to-date ways to exist within that complexity. Certainly, there is an increasing number of technological tools available to support people working together, but is collaboration just about being open to working and sharing with others?

Organizations are living systems, but they go well beyond the biological. A colony of ants may well cooperate in their daily existence, but they do not have the level of consciousness of humans. Organizations are made up of individuals, each with their own complex needs and desires. You can bully and coerce people into doing things and that is one way to get things done. Sadly, some organizations still employ this model. Today, we consider ourselves much more evolved and we require a more evolved way of managing and interacting.

Organizations, and the individuals within them, have the possibility to choose self-determination. In others words, they can decide on a goal and they can embark on the steps to achieve that goal. However, the mental and physical energies required to create change can quickly dissipate if there is no *structured method* to harness those energies in the direction of the goal. Entropy exists and it needs to be addressed.

The Theory of Constraints provides a set of Thinking Processes to guide and structure the planning and implementation of projects toward a goal. Moreover, the more statistically stable (hence predictable) are the work processes underpinning the execution of tasks and the more we understand and manage their variation, the more possibility we have to achieve our goals and grow.

A great deal of effort is being put into discussions and meetings in organizations to arrive at shared intentions. This is undoubtedly important, but we need to go further. For those with an interest in spirituality, there is a parallel we learned from a Rabbi friend: in prayer, intention *(Kavanah)* is important, but not sufficient. You also need structure for that intention to be most effective. And even if the intention is confused, the structure will help make up for that.

Whatever the intentions and goals are for an organization, in order for the people in that organization to work together fruitfully, collaboratively, and fairly, they need to structure their efforts *with method and suitable tools.* This is the best recipe for making your intentions work in an organization. As Dr. Deming would repeatedly say: "Our good will and best efforts are not enough."

How can we then structure our collaborative efforts? How can we mold our good will and efforts to transform them into sustainable results?

Some Help from Network Theory

In the last 15–20 years, the studies in Complexity have unveiled a wealth of commonalities among different phenomena whose understanding is facilitated by Network Theory. From the Internet to condensed matter physics, Network Theory seems to be able to shed a light on what happens when "things start to get together."

Networks are made up of interconnected nodes (through links). There are various kinds of network in the real world. Some occur in nature, such as a beehive. Other networks are manmade, such as the London Underground (Figure 4.1).

These "simple" networks are not designed with a specific goal that affects how the nodes interact with each other. They simply allow connections to occur randomly; hence they are called *random* networks.

The statistical distribution that describes the probability with which these nodes are connected to each other follows a Gaussian-like (bell shaped) distribution.

Line 1

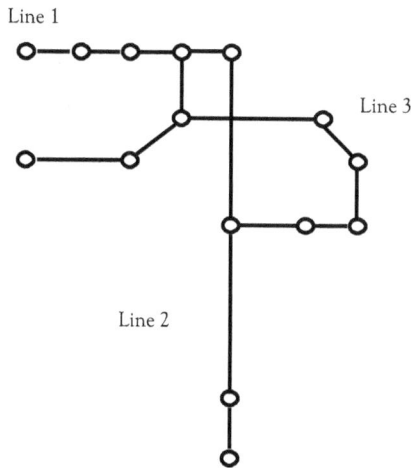

Line 3

Line 2

Figure 4.1 A simple subway network

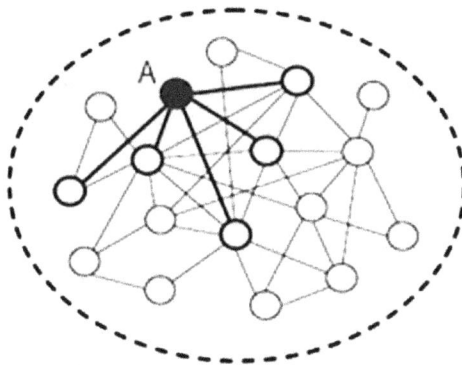

Figure 4.2 A network with a hub

A different kind of network exists where the number of interconnections among the nodes is not distributed around a mean. Some nodes have a much higher number of interconnections than others. The nodes with more nodes connected to them are called *hubs*. These networks, known as *scale-free networks*, thus have a hierarchy based on the frequency with which nodes are visited.

Such a hierarchy of connections can be coherent with the goal that this network is trying to achieve or, as often happens in organizations, can simply be the result of the way informal communities of practices congregate to "get the job done" (Figure 4.2).

Functional Hierarchies in organizations are created out of a Newtonian paradigm of mechanical interactions and, ultimately, they trigger a power game separated from the goal the hierarchy was designed to achieve, the goal of the organization. Hierarchies within scale-free Networks, on the contrary, are what happens when individuals with competencies work together to accomplish a common goal. Said in a different way: *Collaboration is what people with different skills and competencies seek in order to accomplish a common objective and it can be greatly enhanced by a Network-like structure.*

These Networks are also called "oriented"; how can we then "orient" the components of an organizational Network?

We need a *protocol* to lead this Network toward its goal and allow collaboration to take place. The 10 steps of the Decalogue, briefly described in the previous chapter, serve precisely this purpose; they allow us to *measure, design, and manage* organizational systems:

- *Measure*: Throughput-based, operational measurements for the performance of the whole system
- *Design*: a Network-like Organization Design
- *Manage*: Establish statistical methods and finite capacity–based algorithms to synchronize available competencies and resources

The 10 steps of the Decalogue are, then, the protocol to support the Systemic Organization Cartoon (i.e., the organization as a system where interdependencies are designed around a strategically chosen constraint). They represent the way out of the complexity conflict in organizations (Figure 4.3).

When *Deming and Goldratt: The Decalogue* was published, Oded and I did not have a "generic" (universally applicable within a defined realm) solution for Step 7 "Create a suitable management/organizational structure" (Figure 4.4); we did not have a clear-cut answer to what a suitable organizational structure would look like. This solution came much later. Before one can truly appreciate the value of the solution, some preliminary language (and the meaning it creates) must be introduced as we will see in the next chapter.

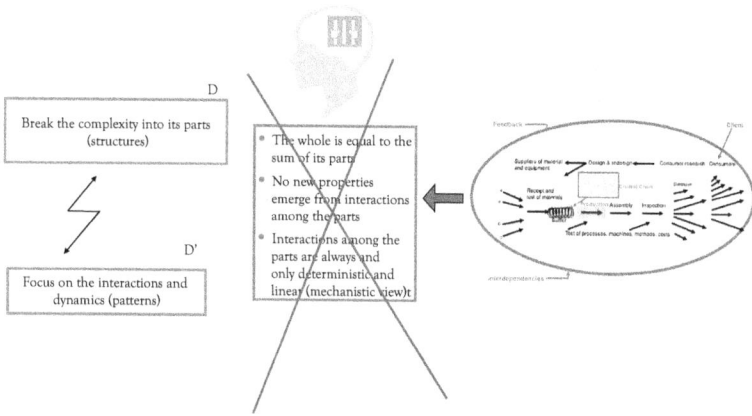

Figure 4.3 The complexity conflict "injected" by the Systemic Organization Cartoon

THE TEN STEPS OF THE DECALOGUE

1. Establish the goal of the System, units of measurement and operational measurement
2. Understand the system (map the interdependencies)
3. Make the system stable (predictable)
4. Build the system around the constraint
5. Manage the constraint -buffer management
6. Reduce variation at (of) the constraint and the main processes
7. **Create a suitable management/organizational structure (network of projects)**
8. Eliminate the "external constraint"—sell all the capacity the system has available
9. Where possible, bring the constraint inside the organization and fix it there
10. Create a program of continuous learning

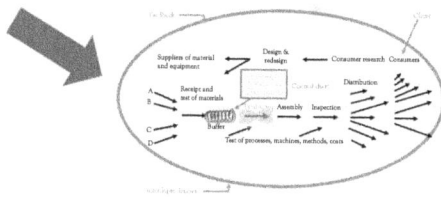

Figure 4.4 The 10 steps of the Decalogue method

Summary of Chapter 4

- Complexity requires new ways to collaborate.
- The thinking processes from the Theory of Constraints can support self-determination in organizations to achieve a goal.
- Entropy exists and people's efforts need to be structured through an appropriate method and tools.

- Network Theory can help us understand how to structure organizations better for collaboration.
- A protocol is required for a network to achieve its goal.
- The 10 steps of the Decalogue provide a protocol that overcomes the complexity conflict.

CHAPTER 5

New Fundamentals of Leadership and Management for the Digital Age

I would say to the House, as I said to those who have joined this government: "I have nothing to offer but blood, toil, tears and sweat."
...You ask, what is our aim? I can answer in one word: It is Victory, victory at all costs, victory in spite of all terror, victory, however long and hard the road may be; for without victory, there is no survival.

—Winston Churchill

If complexity requires new ways to collaborate, as we stated at the beginning of the last chapter, it also brings new considerations for leadership and management.

What is Leadership? Let's be specific. In the context of organizations, it is about empowering people to pursue a shared vision.

A leader must therefore be capable of designing and impressing upon his/her people

(a) The image of a desirable future
(b) Why and how it is possible to achieve it

In his famous 1940 speech to the House of Commons that preceded the rescue operation in Dunkirk, Churchill does precisely this: highlights the Vision ("Victory"), the why ("without Victory there is no survival"), and the how ("Blood, Toil, Sweat and Tears").

In our daily work, we may not face the same dramatic challenges of a war and we may not need the inflammatory rhetoric required for those dark days. But, if we want to pride ourselves with some sort of leadership skills, we must make sure that some of the basics are covered. Indeed, in what follows, we are concerned with leadership for organizations.

First, a leader owns a Theory, a set of well-tested assumptions within a well-defined realm of validity. Without Theory, Management—the activities we do to achieve our vision—becomes a "whack-a-mole" game and finger pointing becomes the rule.

Second, a leader is capable of communicating effectively inside and outside the organization why the Theory will produce the desired results; in other words, the role of the leader is to create predictability of outcome for the efforts he/she requires from their people as well as constancy of purpose among them.

Third, a leader is selfless and relentless in elevating everyone's abilities through continuous teaching and mentoring.

How is all this applicable in the digital age? An analogy may help.

In the early 1980s, American car manufacturers had dramatically lost competitiveness and "Quality" came onto the scene. Quality professionals had a major opportunity to ride the high wave of innovation and systems-based management underpinned by the work of Dr. W. Edwards Deming. Instead, they decided to pummel themselves into irrelevance by hiding behind nonsensical ISO-like quality assurance schemes and surrendering to the statistical hallucinations of six-sigma and Lean.

Their major sin was to think of "continuous improvement," the mantra of Quality Management, as just a set of techniques with no direct connection to business results besides some cost savings.

People involved in leading the development and implementation of digital technologies have a choice: follow the path of the Quality professionals and walk into their own professional cage, or arm themselves with cause-and-effect reasoning and stand up to the challenge.

Software technologies have always been considered, at best, a necessary evil. No Top Executive of a non-tech organization comes from Technology. This is changing rapidly. Digital Strategists now sit at the C-suite table and are called upon to deliver the redesign of their organizations in light of what they can enable business-wise. Digital must no longer simply "support" the business; it must "be" the business because in today's world, every company is a technology company.

The inherent challenge for digital professionals is to "see" the business and be breadwinners. They have a unique opportunity to impact the information and material flows that shape the success of their organization. Digital technology has the possibility to overcome the fallacies of budget-driven, functional silos and to alleviate the predicaments generated by a hierarchical view of the organization.

The starting point to becoming a real leader in the digital age is *understanding how to manage the flow in an organizational system.* As I mentioned in the previous chapter, we need to introduce some new language for a new solution. To manage flow, leaders must grasp some fundamentals: understanding *variation* and why we need a *constraint.*

The Need for a Constraint

Although the word constraint may sound negative, in practice it is not. It turns out that we actually *need* a constraint and that is very useful. This is true for two precise reasons:

1. We need a constraint to facilitate the synchronization of the different processes in the system (the constraint is the element that dictates the pace at which value is generated).
2. We need a constraint because an "unbalanced" system is more solid and it is more easily managed when the impact of variation is taken into account.

In light of the above, we can in fact *choose* the constraint; we decide where it is possible to conveniently (strategically) position the constraint in order to manage it.

Let's see in more detail why an unbalanced system is simpler to manage than a balanced one. The simplest way to exemplify the power that stems from focusing only on one constraint in an organizational system is a production flow. However, this is only *one* example. The production line represented in the following example could just as well represent *all* the processes of an organization, or even *the various elements in an entire supply chain.* It would be a huge disservice to the Theory of Constraints to consider it as something that is restricted to manufacturing and logistics.

Indeed, the following line of reasoning can and has been applied for decades to a myriad of business environments.

A balanced plant or system is a production flow where the process stages (for the sake of simplicity, machines) that generate the finished products all have the same nominal production capacity. The goal of a balanced system (Figure 5.1) is to match the capacity of the various stages so that there is no excess capacity in any part of the system.

Unfortunately, this scenario is quite unrealistic because we are overlooking the impact of variation on the different stages of the chain. At each stage, the amount of production will be affected by variation resulting in the impossibility of the system being "balanced."

Let's look at a simple example.

Let's imagine we have a market demand of 10 units of our product and a production process with 5 stages, where every stage has the same production average and the same amount of variation as the others. On average, every step of the process can produce, and make available to the next step, 10 semifinished units per hour, with a performance that varies within a range from 6 to 14 units.

Let's simulate the first production cycle.

The first stage passes on to the second stage something between 6 and 14 units (let's say 11), the second stage will be able to produce any result between 6 and 14 (let's say 14); similarly, the third stage will generate 8, the fourth stage 12, and the last stage 7.

Given this combination of output, which is perfectly compatible with the machines chosen (by average and variation), how much finished product really comes out at the end of the first production cycle (Figure 5.2)?

The first stage will deliver 11 units to the second stage. The second stage is able to process all 11 units. The third stage will receive the 11

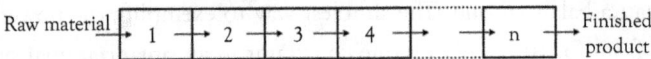

Figure 5.1 A balanced system

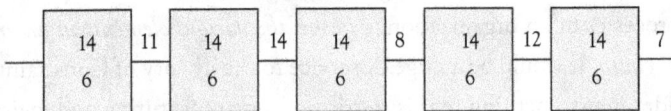

Figure 5.2 First production cycle

units, but, due to *variation*, it will only process 8 of them and pass them on to the fourth stage. The fourth stage has an instantaneous capacity to process 12 units but, as it only received 8, it will only process those and pass them on to the next stage. The last stage has an instantaneous capacity to process only 7 units; consequently, 1 unit will get left behind. The final result is that, after an input of 11 units, only 7 are produced (Figure 5.3).

It is clear that 4 units are somehow "lost" inside the production chain as work in progress (Figure 5.4). In this case, 3 units are stuck between machines 2 and 3 and the other unit between machines 4 and 5:

To summarize, even if the market demand was 10 units, equivalent to our "average capacity," we would not be able to satisfy demand because *interdependencies and variation* make it impossible to "balance" the production.

Under the initial assumptions, let's see what happens as time goes by. Because variation over time is the same (the range is from 6 to 14), and all the stages have the same average value, the second production cycle will be able to use the semifinished units that are still in the system.

Let's look at a simulation of the second cycle:

The first stage will deliver 9 units to the second stage (Figure 5.5). The second stage will be able to process all 9 units. The third stage will receive the

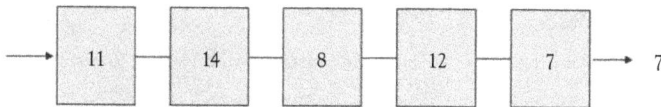

Figure 5.3 Result of first production cycle

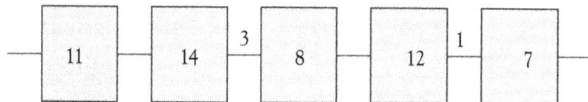

Figure 5.4 Units "lost" inside production chain

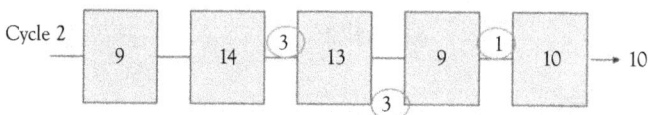

Figure 5.5 Second production cycle

9 units plus the 3 semifinished already present in the system and will process all of them and pass them on to the fourth stage. The fourth stage is able to process 9 units, leaving behind 3 semifinished units. The last stage will use these 9 units, plus the 1 already present as WIP, ending the cycle with 10 units produced and 3 left in front of the penultimate processing stage.

As the system is made up of a series of *interdependent bottlenecks*, in every single cycle, the instantaneous production capacity of the entire production flow will be equal to the capacity of the stage that has produced the minimum capacity. Moreover, as every machine has a capacity that varies above and below 10 units per cycle, it is almost certain that at least one of the machines has an instantaneous capacity that is less than the average value. Therefore, the real capacity of the entire system will always be something less than 10 units per cycle, at least as long as the stages are interdependent. We are in a paradoxical situation where we produce WIP without managing to satisfy market demand (10 units/cycle).

As production continues (the number of cycles increases), there is an increase in the semifinished material that accumulates between one production stage and another; this is due to the effect of variation in each stage and goes on until the production stages become *decoupled*. Now no stage is forced to remain inactive and each stage can operate independently from the previous one, with a global capacity that is close to its own average value.

The price of decoupling is an increase in WIP (Inventory); this means keeping money frozen within the system (Figure 5.6).

With a balanced process, we can deliver 100 percent of market demand *only* if these two conditions are met at the same time:

- We accept to size the process so that the market demand for every cycle is considerably less than the average value of the production capacity for each stage.

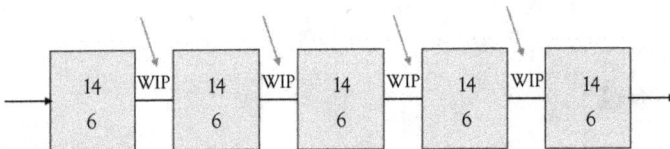

Figure 5.6 Increase in semifinished material

- We wait for the condition of decoupling of the production stages to happen.

These conditions allow us to deliver 100 percent of the demand, without generating too much WIP, only by having a much greater production capacity in every stage compared to actual demand. In our example, the system would be able to deliver 100 percent of market demand if this demand was 8–9 units/cycle (considerably lower than the average of 10 units/cycle).

A different approach is to increase the capacity of some of the stages of the production process so that there is always *only one limiting stage (constraint)* in the flow of material (Figure 5.7).

This choice allows us to eliminate most of the WIP, as long as the capacity of the constraint (and therefore of the other stages) is sized on the basis of market demand (market demand must be equal to the average production capacity of the constraint). Also, the flow of the material has to be managed around the constraint; this strategy also foresees an oversizing of production capacity, but it also has a number of advantages.

Instead of balancing the system, and then trying to improve it by balancing it and reducing variation in all the production stages, we apply the Theory of Constraints (TOC) solution. After identifying (or choosing) the constraint, we manage the system around the constraint itself. With this solution, we "unbalance" the system because it is simpler and cheaper to manage.

In an unbalanced system, everything revolves around the constraint phase and there are many advantages to this. A detailed plan is made for this phase only. This schedule allows us to manage the whole production system. Also, reducing (global) variation in an unbalanced system means concentrating on and investing in the constraint phase only, not in every single part of the production process. Consequently, increasing the productivity and improving the performance of an unbalanced plant is considerably cheaper and less wasteful in terms of time and energy.

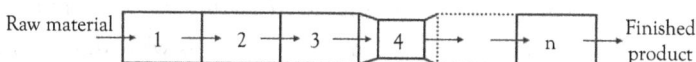

Figure 5.7 *The constraint in the flow of material*

The algorithm that embodies this approach to the synchronized scheduling of finite capacity, which has been largely used by a multiplicity of industries all around the world for more than 30 years, is called "Drum–Buffer–Rope" (DBR); it is a three-step process:

1. We identify/choose the constraint.
2. We exploit the constraint.
3. We subordinate the system to the constraint.

To be more specific, first *we identify the constraint* in the cycle, and then we decide to manage it effectively. Managing the constraint effectively means managing it so it never stops: in other words, it must never be "starved" of input. In TOC, this is called *exploiting the constraint.*

For this exploitation to happen, every other stage/process in the system has to *subordinate.* This means that there must be enough production capacity upstream to always produce semi-finished units to feed the constraint continuously and enough production capacity downstream to guarantee that what the constraint produces can be processed. Statistically speaking, this means that the "ranges of variation" upstream and downstream of the constraint phase must have a lower limit of oscillation that is greater than the upper limit of the constraint phase.

As far as WIP is concerned, whereas in the case of the balanced system it must be available in front of *all of* the production stages so that uncoupling can occur, in the case of the system with a constraint, WIP must only accumulate in front of the constraint stage to keep it continuously fed. What is more, if the material is released to the whole plant at the pace at which the constraint can process it, the amount of WIP needed to achieve optimal performance can also be kept to the minimum.

Protecting the Constraint: The "Buffer"

The algorithm we have just described has the aim of maximizing the performance of the system and it is totally dependent on the correct and continuous functioning of the constraint. Managing the constraint effectively implies that it must never "starve" and that is why we must have some kind of protection mechanism in place. In TOC, the protection mechanism is called "buffer management." In a system that is unbalanced

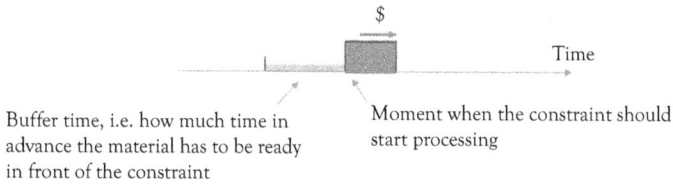

Buffer time, i.e. how much time in advance the material has to be ready in front of the constraint

Moment when the constraint should start processing

Figure 5.8 Buffer time

around the constraint and subordinated to it, the buffer protects the constraint from variation. The unit of measurement of the buffer is *time* (Figure 5.8).

Once we know the amount of variation the constraint is affected by (both in terms of input it receives and its processing time), we can define how much time in advance the material has to be ready in front of it. The final, and most important, step is to *manage the buffer*. Essentially, we have to have an operational procedure that supports our decision-making process; in order to be sure that the constraint works all the time, we have to guarantee that the buffer is never reduced to zero.

Since we believe that statistical predictability is the foundation of management, we must monitor the consumption of the buffer statistically and act accordingly. If the consumption is "statistically stable," we do not intervene; *vice versa*, if the consumption is statistically unstable, then we must take action.

Summary of Chapter 5

- Leadership is about empowering people to pursue a shared vision. A leader must therefore be capable of designing and impressing upon his/her people (a) the image of a desirable future and (b) *why* and *how* it is possible to achieve it.
- A leader is someone who
  (a) owns a Theory, a set of well-tested assumptions within a well-defined realm of validity. Without Theory, Management—that activity we do to achieve our vision—becomes a "whack-a-mole" game and finger pointing becomes the rule.
  (b) is capable of communicating effectively inside and outside the organization why the Theory will produce the desired results; in other words, the role of the leader is to create *predictability of*

outcome for the efforts he/she requires from their people as well as *constancy of purpose* among them.

(c) is selfless and relentless in elevating everyone's abilities through continuous teaching and mentoring.

- The starting point to become a real leader in the digital age is understanding how to manage the flow in an organizational system.
- Some management fundamentals for managing flow are understanding variation and why we need a constraint.
- Variation affects all human processes and it needs to be understood and managed.
- Statistical predictability is the foundation of management.
- A constraint is a positive thing because we can use it to facilitate the synchronization of the different processes in the system (the constraint is the element that dictates the pace at which value is generated).
- We need a constraint because an "unbalanced" system is more solid and it is more easily managed when the impact of variation is taken into account.
- It makes no sense to run a "balanced" plant because at each stage, the amount of production will be affected by *variation*, resulting in the impossibility of the system being "balanced."
- In a system that is unbalanced around the constraint and subordinated to it, we use a *buffer* to protect the constraint from variation. The unit of measurement of the buffer is *time*.

CHAPTER 6

Speeding Up for Technology

Technology, by design or not, pushes the boundaries of what is possible. In doing so, it opens up new cognitive realms and provides new perspectives. The speed at which it progresses is much greater than our ability, as humans, to adapt to the changes it brings along. Technology is *de facto* dictating the pace of our "evolution," and schools, institutions, and industries frequently fail to grasp its transformational, sociological, and neuro-psychological content.

Some technologies, to use a popular term, are "disruptive"; they alter the existing paradigm so much, so quickly, and so abruptly that entire sectors are bowled over by them.

Digital is, by all means, one of these technologies: IoT, AI, Industry 4.0, etc. are all messengers of a new world in which closer integration of value chains is paramount.

As we said before, digital heralds the transition from a worldview centered on "atoms" to one based on "zeros and ones." One of its most intriguing, paradigm-altering developments is Blockchain. So far, the debate has been almost exclusively around one and only one application: Crypto-Currencies. Bitcoin and the likes have been stealing the show and shifted the debate away from where I believe it should be.

About 10 years ago, in a white paper signed by Satoshi Nakamoto (nobody seems to know if the person really exists; he/she may be the Homer of our millennium and the paper his/her boringly technical Odyssey), a new possibility for digital emerged: bypass the omnipresent power of clearing houses in economic transactions.

Immediately, people interested in speculating (or simply conducting dodgy activities) started to swarm to the arena of crypto, boosting a delirious debate around the concept of currency and the role of Central Banks. I will not get into that (and the dangers of pegging a currency to something that glitters and could be "mined").

It is the implications of this technology, instead, that are society-altering. What Blockchain seems to be able to do is not just bypass the nonvalue-added (and expensive) activities of a bank, allowing peer-to-peer transactions; what it promises is the possibility to build *a whole new, higher level of value to the chains that deliver products and services*. It creates trust by ensuring transparency and accountability in all phases of complex chains of value (provided that the majority of the nodes of the network are not controlled by "bad guys").

This will directly impact the way organizations are structured. Such trust, "guaranteed" by contracts that promise to be "smart," does indeed go hand in hand with alternative forms of organizational structures that are not conventionally hierarchical. Many alternatives that are being proposed mirror some biological phenomena, such as "ecosystems" or "self-organizing systems." The word "Holon," in all its declinations, seems to have gained ample consensus among the advocates of a different way of organizing people's work. Holacracy is an example. In the last few years, nonhuman forms of leadership such as DAO (Decentralized Autonomous Organizations) also seem to be gaining traction.

Needless to say, computer Leviathans such as IBM and SAP are all over Blockchain. It is paradoxical that very rigid, Command and Control, cost-centered giants seem to be promoting a different design for work … putting "lipstick on the pig," to quote a sorely missed leader from Chicago. Succumbing to the mirage of a life-saving technology that echoes the glory days of picks and shovels (mining) still seems to have an allure. Perhaps this is because deep-seated images always trump the thinking process. Unfortunately, the issue of redesigning our organizations for the digital age to truly reap the advantages of promising technologies is not (simply) a topological one. It is something that goes well beyond the surface.

Redesigning Organizations for the Digital Age

When Dr. Deming was asked to comment on the latest "Quality Improvement Technique" as an allegedly "practical" way to promote Quality, he would inevitably respond: "Let's go back to serious business." So let's.

If *Quality* (low variation of all processes and focus on the customer), *Involvement* (the intrinsic motivation generated by people's job satisfaction and alignment on the goal), and *Flow* (how we arrange for products, services, information, and money to move through the organization and along the chains the organizations are part of) are the hallmarks for a transition toward a truly Systemic Organization, then we have to design for that and abandon any bio-computational fantasies.

Where is a good place to start to build a successful organization? A group of people, bound by a commonly agreed goal, who are asked to lend their competencies and ingenuity for the achievement of that goal in exchange for a fair compensation and a climate that nurtures their desire to learn and be part of something meaningful and bigger than themselves I think it is a good start.

What this group of people needs is a structured way of communicating, cooperating, and progressing toward their goal within a statistically predictable timeframe, an agreed-upon budget, and in full compliance with their client's needs. In English (and in many other languages, I am confident) there is a precise word for this kind of arrangement: Project.

Accordingly, if we want to be minimally credible in our desire to bring about all the undeniable advantages put forth by the marvels of the digital age, we must reconcile the project-like nature of collaborative work with the way this work is led and managed and how its results are measured.

Before we get into semantic trouble, we must understand what we mean by *Processes* and *Projects*.

Processes, Projects, and Managing Projects with Critical Chain

We believe that any serious conversation about "systems thinking" when it comes to managing organizations must start from acknowledging that a system is a network of interdependent processes (the basic components of the system) that work together for a common goal.

A process is what transforms an input into an output; such a process, no matter how complex, innovative, mental, or physical, has a beginning and an end; it has a viable temporal span for its execution, a variation that must be managed, and it requires resources. If we accept the idea that resources, human and material, are finite and their role is to maximize their contribution to the overall chosen and accepted goal of the system, then having a metric in place can only be beneficial. If we choose a metric that cohesively integrates resources and time, then we have Projects that we can schedule with some hope of success, which means that can realistically be on time, in specs, and within budget.

In his 1997 business novel *Critical Chain*, Dr. Goldratt casts a new light on the controversial issue of managing finite resources in a project environment by offering a radically different view of how projects should be scheduled and how their execution should be managed. By leveraging the concept of covariance and presenting a powerful finite capacity algorithm, he redefines the rules for successful Project Management.

Traditional project management methods using a critical path cannot guarantee that projects are completed on time, according to specs, and within budget. The shortcomings of project management were examined by Dr. Goldratt in *Critical Chain*, where he presents a profound innovation for reliable management of projects. Traditional PM is often based on an assumption of infinite capacity and therefore can lead to resource contention.

The traditional critical path method is plagued by wrong-thinking and wrong habits, such as multitasking and "student syndrome,"—putting off tasks until the last minute—that can slow projects down artificially. The Critical Chain method tackles head-on many of the issues that prevent projects from completing successfully by

(a) eliminating milestones; instead the entire project is protected with a buffer at the end (project buffer) to protect from accumulated variation;

(b) making realistic assessments of task length instead of adding protection to each task, thus speeding up the project;

(c) resolving resource contention by allowing for finite capacity by calculating the Critical Chain, i.e., the longest sequence of dependent events *taking into consideration the sharing of resources*. This sequence determines the length of the project, and this is the limiting factor (constraint) of the project itself (Figure 6.1).

(d) Noncritical branches, called feeders, are also protected with a cumulative buffer (not individually) placed at the end of the "feeding chain."

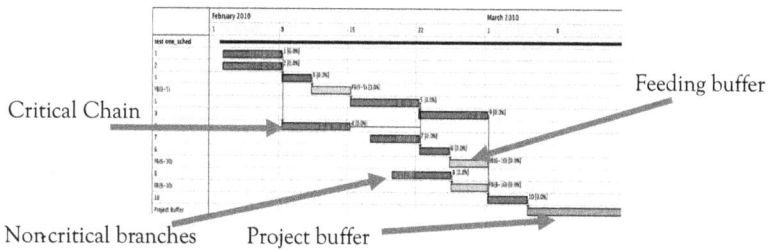

Figure 6.1 The critical chain of a project

Critical Chain and Organizational Design

Critical Chain is much more than simply an algorithm to accelerate project completion; it is the vehicle to integrate, control, and deploy the resources of the organization. In this way, *the Critical Chain algorithm also provides the foundation for the redesign of organizations.*

In the process of our work over the last two decades, we have come to understand how organizations in their entirety can be seen as *networks made up of Processes and Projects*; some of these processes will be very repetitive and easily managed, DFC and Process Behavior Charts will suffice; some others will be more innovative, have a higher level of complexity, and will require a more comprehensive management approach, i.e., a Critical Chain project management schedule and an execution plan.

Process Behavior Charts for essentially repetitive processes and the Critical Chain approach to the management of projects provide all the *profound knowledge*, as well as the holistic measurement and control mechanisms, to transition safely from the largely obsolete Hierarchical/Functional organizational design to a very "all hands on deck" systemic model.

Summary of Chapter 6

- The speed at which technology progresses is far greater than our ability, as humans, to adapt to the changes it brings along.
- The implications of new technologies are society-altering.
- The issue of redesigning our organizations for the digital age to truly reap the advantages of promising technologies is not (simply) a topological one. We need to understand that the work of organizations is made up of processes and projects.

- We must reconcile the project-like nature of collaborative work with the way this work is led and managed and how its results are measured.
- Critical Chain Project Management is much more than simply an algorithm to accelerate project completion; it is the vehicle to integrate, control, and deploy the resources of the organization. In this way, *the Critical Chain algorithm also provides the foundation for the redesign of organizations.*
- Process Behavior Charts and the Critical Chain approach to the management of projects provide the *profound knowledge* and holistic measurement and control mechanisms to transition safely from the Hierarchical/Functional organizational design to a systemic model.

CHAPTER 7

Optimizing Resources and Technologies Through the Organization as a Network of Projects

The implication of Network Theory for organizations is profound; when we examine an organization in this light, we can see that there is an inherent network-like nature, and we can analyze its behavior and development with new understanding. More importantly, this knowledge allows us to consciously *design, manage, and operate the organization* with a much higher level of optimization, overcoming silos and artificial barriers. This will inevitably accelerate flow and also the successful adoption of new technologies. This optimization is not only relevant for organizations but entire supply chains. We have come to call this organizational model the Network of Projects.

Proposing the Organizational Design of the Networks of Projects

A network is a set of "nodes" connected by "links"; it is not a static entity, indeed it is something that continuously evolves, and its sustainable development is governed by a dynamic dictated by the emergence of a few hubs strongly connected to nodes through links whose behavior is statistically predictable. This dynamic is, especially in the specific case of human networks, nonlinear because of the intrinsic nonlinearity of the interactions between the nodes (people or groups of people).

At the most fundamental level, organizations are networks of different communities of practices; it seems only reasonable that the prevailing silo-based, hierarchical/functional organizational design be replaced with an organic way of structuring such practices. First, in *Sechel: Logic, Language and Tools to Manage Any Organization as a Network* (Intelligent Management Inc., 2011), followed by our chapter for Springer, "Managing Complexity in Organizations Through a Systemic Network of Projects" (2015) and then more comprehensively in *Quality, Involvement, Flow: The Systemic Organization* (CRC Press, 2016) my colleagues and I presented a new model for the sustainable growth of organizations based on the concept of a *Network of Projects*. A Network of Projects leverages the power of the Critical Chain algorithm developed by Dr. Goldratt to build organizational systems where control mechanisms, feedback cycles, and rational allocation of finite resources are more effective and in line with the goals of the organization.

Everything that an organization does can be thought of in terms of a project. Some projects, like bookkeeping, are repetitive, and others, like developing a new product, introducing a new technology, or launching a new marketing campaign, are non-repetitive. These projects are a network. In Chapter 4, we looked briefly at Network Theory. The Network of Projects that makes up the life of the organization is a particular kind of Network, called *directed* network, where the "direction" is provided by the goal of the organization. Such networks are called *scale free*, with a hierarchy of hubs and nodes. Accordingly, in an organization, there will be *hub-projects*, namely the ones more relevant for the success of the organization, and "node-projects," projects that are smaller but still necessary for the development of the organizational network. What ensures the connection among these Hub and Node Projects is the finite capacity algorithm for their synchronization, fueled by an appropriate Database of resources. Within the 10 steps of the Decalogue for managing organizations as systems, based on managing variation and constraints, Step 7 regarding organizational design becomes the design of a Network of Projects.

Optimizing Resources and Technologies

A Network of Projects leverages the power of the Critical Chain algorithm developed by Dr. Goldratt to build organizations as systems where control mechanisms, feedback cycles, and rational allocation of finite resources are more effective and in line with the goals of the organization.

Designing and managing an organization as a systemic network of projects allows us to overcome the strictures that interfere with performance resulting from the artificial divisions of a traditional hierarchy/function style of management. The activities carried out in any organization need to be staffed with people with suitable *competencies*. It will be very cumbersome to deploy these competencies in a timely and systemic way if we organize them functionally. Why? Because any attempt to use a resource allocated to "Function A" to perform its competence beyond the boundaries of its Function will immediately result in a conflict between the head of the Function and whoever has been given the task to deploy that competence, usually a project manager. Unfortunately, virtually every minimally complex activity needed by any company to achieve any goal is cross-functional in nature, hence we are stuck in a real dilemma about how to best utilize the resources at hand. This dilemma is particularly felt by CIOs and CDOs attempting to roll out technologies end to end across an entire organization. The more we realize how paralyzing this dilemma is, the closer we come to understanding the paradigm shift needed to create organizations that are not suboptimized.

The clash between a functional organization and achieving cross-functional goals is, quite plainly and simply, what keeps organizations stuck. This dilemma is the chronic conflict that keeps the science of management from evolving into the real engine of economic growth. Addressing the multilayered issue of how to optimize finite resources to maximize Throughput is critical if we are to generate wealth sustainably.

So what happens if we view the recurrent and non-recurrent activities in an organization as "projects"? Whether we seek to improve the speed at which we develop and manufacture new products, install new equipment, organize shipments, or file quarterly closing, we need the *coordinated and synchronized efforts* of many different competencies. Deploying these competencies in a logical sequence is relatively easy. However, breaking assumptions about the way performances should be controlled and measured seems to be a true cognitive ordeal. The measurement of performances seems to be inextricably connected with a local, i.e., functional, indicator whereas we all know that what matters is the *global bottom line* of the company. How do we come out of this seemingly irreconcilable conflict? We do so by asking ourselves what company functions are for, and uncovering the obvious truth that functions *should house competencies, not fiefdoms.*

Engineers, accountants, scientists, subject matter experts should not be considered members of a "company function." Rather, they should be seen as valuable *competencies* that can be deployed for the goal of the whole company. These resources, ALL the resources, should be available for whatever "project" the company needs to accomplish.

What kind of control mechanism can we rely on in a Network of Projects? Project buffers not only provide the control mechanism to protect against disruption, but also give us statistical understanding of project development and early warnings on potential delays and are normally measured in *time*. Simply put, buffers cumulate protection from variation associated with the execution of every task. In this way, they provide a time "shield" against delay.

The statistical property that buffers leverage is called covariance; let's say that it is a very efficient way to "pool" time.

How About Money?

A company viewed as a Network of Projects is a natural evolution of W. Edwards Deming's original 1952 system design. Each project is protected with a time buffer. Success in project execution is measured in terms of timeliness, adherence to specs, and cash outlay; the first two are peculiar to each project, but cash can be pooled to protect the entire Network of Projects.

Said in a different way, the money buffer that protects each project from variation in cash outlay (typically, Totally Variable Costs, TVC— the subset of the inventory that goes into a project) could be pooled in a buffer that protects ALL the projects. Covariance holds for money too.

The rationale for this choice is mathematically obvious, less so its organizational implications. Pooling resources is a systemic concept; it comes from a paradigm of whole system optimization and the reconciliation of the inherent conflict between Local *vs.* Global performance measurement.

Pooling cash to protect the entirety of the network of projects (enabling maximization of results) is possible only if we abandon the idea of "functional budgeting" and cost centers. We can take intelligent decisions about how we invest our money only if we take intelligent decisions about how we want to work.

Critical Chain as the Engine of a Systemic Organization

What we are saying is that *any company should be seen as a network of projects with the global goal of maximizing the Throughput of the company.* The theme of Goldratt's book *Critical Chain* is that we can maximize the speed of new product development by adopting a particular approach to Project Management (PM). The implications of that approach are truly far reaching and pave the way for a complete and yet largely unexplored solution to the inherent conflict of any organization (hierarchy *vs.* no hierarchy).

What we have been able to discover in over 20 years of implementing the Decalogue is that the Critical Chain method that Dr. Goldratt developed can be used not only to maximize the use of the finite resources of a company; this algorithm can be used to redesign the way any company works. Critical Chain becomes, then, much more than simply an algorithm to accelerate project completion; *it is the vehicle to integrate, control, and deploy the resources of the organization.*

What does the network of projects organization look like? Instead of company functions, there are networks of projects; instead of heads of functions, there are managers of increasingly complex projects that draw their resources *from a pool of available competencies* with no resource contention; instead of executives that fight for power, there is cooperative work that is in synch with the goal of the company. Instead of often-conflicting local indicators of performance, there is one single driver for everybody. An organization as a network is part of a network of networks. This realization, and the shift in mindset it requires, open up new opportunities and possibilities beyond individual companies for *collaboration along entire supply chains.*

The Network of Conversations in Organizations

The links that connect the elements of an organization, are the *conversations for action* that take place. The effective synchronization of these conversations is possible only if the basic processes that these conversations represent are statistically predictable in their outcomes. The question then becomes, how can we make the outcome of conversations predictable? How can we frame a human interaction based on language (as opposed to a one-way command to a machine) in a way that leads to predictable and actionable outcomes?

We can replace the outdated Hierarchical/Functional structure with a much more organic design, based on managing variation and constraints, that reflects the intrinsically project-like nature of the work of organizations. This change is not cosmetic, it is transformational and it is rooted in a paradigm of cooperation, togetherness, and win–win. The new covenant that everyone in the organization—as well as the *value chain* in which the organization is embedded—must embrace requires a much higher ability to think, communicate, and act; it requires a new "wiring" in the way we measure, manage, and sustainably improve our efforts toward our goals.

The real challenge in bringing about a transformation based on a Network of Projects lies in the *emotional and cognitive shift* that needs to occur in the way people learn and use their knowledge as well as how they see themselves develop and interact in the workplace. The Thinking Processes from the Theory of Constraints were developed by Dr. Goldratt to aid that shift (we take a look at these in Chapter 10). Far from being a mere technique, we have found them to be a critical element in transforming organizations into "thinking systems" because they foster in people the ability to see interdependencies, resolve conflicts, be empowered, work cooperatively, communicate effectively, and, at a higher level, perceive (and act consistently with) the oneness of the organization with its business and physical environment.

To replace successfully a traditional Hierarchy with a Network of Projects, we need to start from the very foundation of how we think, speak, and act. What we need to learn is how to seamlessly connect our uniquely human abilities to

(a) Systematically develop solutions to seemingly insurmountable conflicts (intuition)
(b) Understand the full spectrum of these solutions (analysis/understanding)

(c) Develop and implement a cohesive and coherent action plan to implement the solutions (knowledge)

(d) Sustain the development of the "intelligent emotions" needed to harness complexity

The Thinking Processes from the Theory of Constraints

With the accelerating complexity in all environments, humans have an unprecedented need to develop the intellectual and emotional skills to navigate change and adapt on a continuous basis. Any organization that wants to continue to go beyond simple survival and prosper needs to find a way to navigate the intellectual and emotional demands of ongoing change.

The Thinking Processes were developed by Dr. Goldratt to sustain and focus the change process underpinned by the process of ongoing improvement at the heart of the Theory of Constraints. Goldratt identified three major phases of change:

1. What to change
2. What to change to
3. How to make the change happen

Goldratt created the Thinking Processes to support and facilitate each of the three phases. He did so as he realized how important it was to provide a strong cognitive support to combat the difficulties associated with change that people inevitably experience. Used as a complete suite, the Thinking Processes have proved themselves to be an effective way to supervise and guide the change process. They are also an ideal companion for developing project plans.

Using precise verbalization and simple diagrams, the Thinking Processes help people to visualize the complex, highly nonlinear network of cause–effect relationships that mark reality, as we perceive it. They allow us to map the "conversations" that make up our cognitive horizon, and these conversations are in themselves a kind of network. Without them, we have no way of grasping the reality of this network, how it defines the semantic boundary of our universe, and how it shapes our actions.

Learning to use the Thinking Processes takes some practice, but within days, they allow people to focus and accelerate their work together. Over time, they enhance and fortify the faculties of the intellect that are responsible for the conception of new ideas (intuition), their full development through analysis (understanding), and the operational deployment of the actions needed to carry out the implementation of the fully analyzed idea (knowledge).

By linking these faculties, the Thinking Processes enable a higher level of control over the interdependencies among these faculties, and this can often lead to conceiving breakthroughs that did not previously seem possible. They also have an important role in reducing variation in our thought processes by focusing our mental efforts toward a goal. They can greatly reduce variation in the way people communicate in an organization by providing a common language. Moreover, they help to harness the powerful forces represented by the emotions involved in the change process, and reinforce and engender the empathy required for collaborative work.

The learning required through a change process can be very destabilizing because it continuously pushes forward the limits of our cognition. It creates a gap between what we know and what we feel we can do, and this gap can be uncomfortable. In order to leverage the tension resulting from this gap in a positive way, we need to understand our emotions better and refine them. In this way, we can transform their potentially destructive power into a positive force for change. The Thinking Processes help people to manage the interdependency of intellect and emotion in the change process. In this way, change can become the transformational effort that is required for any sustainable, as opposed to temporary, shift. We will look at them in more detail in Chapter 10.

Shifting Beyond the Hierarchical Mindset

The major problem with replacing a hierarchical mindset lies in the subliminal, unchallenged mental models that make us believe that an organization requires a superimposed control mechanism, be it a boss, a function, or an accounting structure based on cost accounting type considerations. The Thinking Processes help us understand the connections, linkages, and the overall mechanism by which we infer reality. Reality is shaped in our minds by connections that largely remain unchallenged unless we unveil them. By making explicit the cause–effect relationships with which we perceive reality, we have an opportunity to challenge all of those assumptions that limit our ability, for instance, to work within a non-silo infrastructure like a network of projects.

More in general, the good functioning of an organization where conventional hierarchy has been challenged lies in enabling higher forms of systemic thinking that are stifled by both current educational systems organized into silos and the corporate world. It is not enough simply to change processes. Flat organizations could easily turn into a short-lived gimmick unless we systemically challenge working and, ultimately, existential paradigms governing the image that we have of what it means to live and work together. This requires a considerable cognitive effort and, without the right cognitive tools to support that effort, there can be little guarantee of continued success (Figure 7.1).

Achieving So Much More

Network theory teaches us that the interaction of hubs and nodes gives birth to emergent properties, i.e., structures or behaviors that emerge spontaneously from interaction. The years of implementations have shown us that we can consider the Decalogue as an emergent property—something that goes far beyond the simple combining of two separate elements. It is a unique methodology that lays the foundations for continuous improvement and sustainable growth and points at a new organizational model. This organizational model evolves the systemic combination of Deming and Goldratt into the design of the network of projects—a vision and a method that can make the systemic organization truly operational. To achieve this reality requires a higher form of intelligence and ethical awareness. We can achieve this with the ecology of the mind that systemic thinking provides and by embracing the values of a worldview where profit and the common good are inextricably interdependent. Both W. Edwards Deming and Eliyahu Goldratt understood that humanity is capable of so much more than we imagine. Whatever situation or business we are in, we can do fundamentally more, and we

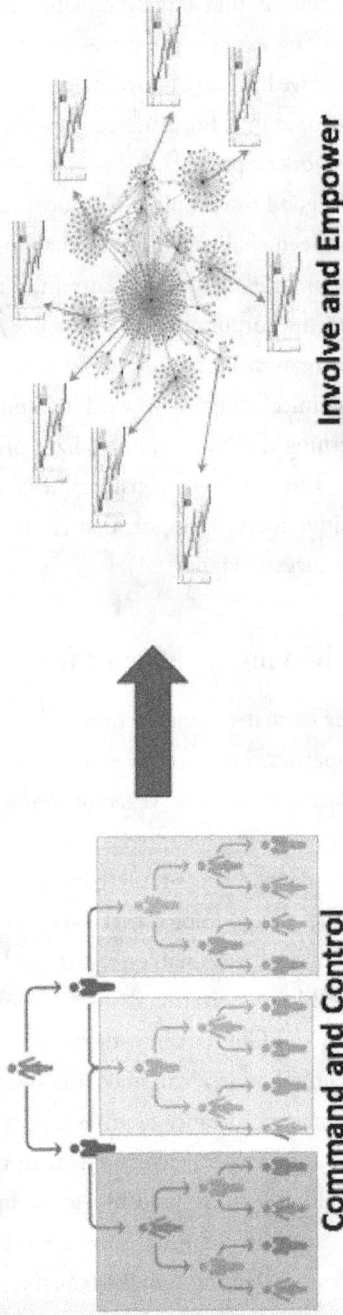

Command and Control

Involve and Empower

Figure 7.1 The shift from command and control to a network of projects

can achieve that in a meaningful way, not to the detriment of others, but by creating something new, better, and from which all will benefit, all through the value chain from the supplier to the end user. Far from being a utopia, this understanding is rapidly becoming the obvious solution, because it is the only sustainable way ahead.

Summary of Chapter 7

- Organizations are inherently network-like in their nature.
- Network theory helps us analyze the behavior and development of organizations with new understanding.
- The knowledge we gain from Network theory allows us to consciously design, manage, and operate the organization with a much higher level of optimization. We have come to call this organizational model the Network of Projects.
- A Network of Projects leverages the power of the Critical Chain algorithm developed by Dr. Goldratt to build organizations as systems where control mechanisms, feedback cycles, and rational allocation of finite resources are more effective and in line with the goals of the organization.
- This change is transformational and is rooted in a paradigm of cooperation, togetherness, and win–win. It requires a much higher ability to think, communicate, and act; it requires a new "wiring" in the way we measure, manage, and sustainably improve our efforts toward our goals.
- The real challenge in bringing about a transformation based on a Network of Projects lies in the *emotional and cognitive shift required.*
- The Thinking Processes from the Theory of Constraints provide an important support for the transformation and help people to manage the interdependency of intellect and emotion in the change process.
- The main challenge in replacing a hierarchical mindset lies in mental models that make us believe that an organization requires a superimposed control mechanism. Shifting mindset requires adequate cognitive tools.

- We can achieve so much more with the ecology of the mind that systemic thinking provides and by embracing the values of a worldview where profit and the common good are inextricably interdependent. This is the only sustainable way ahead.

CHAPTER 8

The Issue of Control and Curing Silo Sickness

It should be clear by now that if we want our organizations to take full advantage of digital technology and build chains of greater value, we need to redesign them to do so. However, let's keep it real: leaders will *only* entertain the notion of redesigning their organization for higher Quality of processes and products, proactive and systematic Involvement of their people, and accelerated Flow of information, products, and money *if* they feel that in the new world they can retain sufficient "control."

Control and Vision in the Decision-Making Process

Control and Vision are two undeniable needs that must always be satisfied. These needs are common to individuals as well as organizations and they take on different verbalizations when focused on specific, practical applications.

Control is something that has to do with the here and now as well as what will happen in the future. Control can be about restricting and dominating things, and the more we feel threatened, the more we feel that we must keep a tight grip. Having control gives us a sense of stability and security. In certain situations, control is connected with confining things in a way that others cannot "interfere." In other situations, control can mean not entering into areas that we feel can destabilize us.

Vision, unlike control which is associated with contraction, is about expansion. It's what makes us get up in the morning. It's about pursuing or achieving what we feel is intimately connected with who we are. Vision connects us with participating in something that is bigger than we are, and by doing so we achieve something that is uniquely human.

The question is, how do "control" and "vision" translate in the decision-making process? A decision point is where we are confronted with the possibility of change. Whether we are cognizant of it or not, every day we make a myriad of decisions; these decisions foreshadow in our mind a "change," hence trigger a conscious decision point, only when we feel that by changing we alter irreversibly the current state of reality AND we are in some way uncomfortable in the current state. In other words, we truly feel the need to make a "life-changing" decision only when the current state of our reality shows some or many elements of discomfort. On the other hand, regardless of our current situation, our innate drive toward elevation and improvement will push us toward wanting to make life-changing decisions.

In this process, "control" takes the shape of "security" and this need leads to *not making the change*; "vision," on the other hand, will be translated as "satisfaction" and will gear our decision toward *making* that change (Figure 8.1).

The Change *vs.* Don't Change conflict is an *archetypal* conflict. In other words, it can be relevant to a wide variety of situations with different verbalizations that in their essence boil down to "Change *vs.* Don't change."

The decision process takes us, then, to a very precise and fundamental dilemma: Change *vs.* Don't change. This dilemma is originated by the two core needs of "control" and "vision" that in the decision process can be verbalized as "security" and "satisfaction."

Let's think about this in relation to the very fundamental Hierarchy *vs.* No Hierarchy Conflict we saw in Chapter 3. As we saw before, the conflict is obvious. On the one hand:

A hierarchy fails to acknowledge three critical aspects of the life of a successful company: interdependencies, feedback cycle, and the customer. For these reasons, it is not suitable for sustaining a continuous improvement effort.

On the other hand: A hierarchy seems to cater for accountability and provides a sense of *control*.

The conflict rests, then, on the idea of control and how this idea is translated into a consistent, and consistently measured, organizational system.

Let's see if I can shed some light on the issue. Leaders of conventional Hierarchies, wittingly or subliminally, view control as an activity

Change Don't Change Conflict

Assumption A-B
- The future is threatened by a lack of control
- Loss of control threatens security

A
Goal
Work towards a desirable future

Assumption A-C
The drive toward the future is triggered by satisfaction

B
Need
Achieve security

C
Need
Pursue satisfaction

Assumption B-D
Stability/continuity are preserved by our current way of acting/thinking

D
Position
Don't change

Assumption C-D'
- A satisfying future cannot only be a repetition of the past
- Any form of the future is associated with change

D'
Conflicting position
Change

Assumptions D-D'
- Any form of change is legitimate and acceptable
- Change can be avoided
- We lose ourselves when we change
- A comfort zone exists, it is an effective way to protect yourself, and it has a precise topography, i.e., it can't be modified in a planned way
- The comfort zone defines who we are
- Things that have worked in the past will work in the future
- The future is something that happens to us

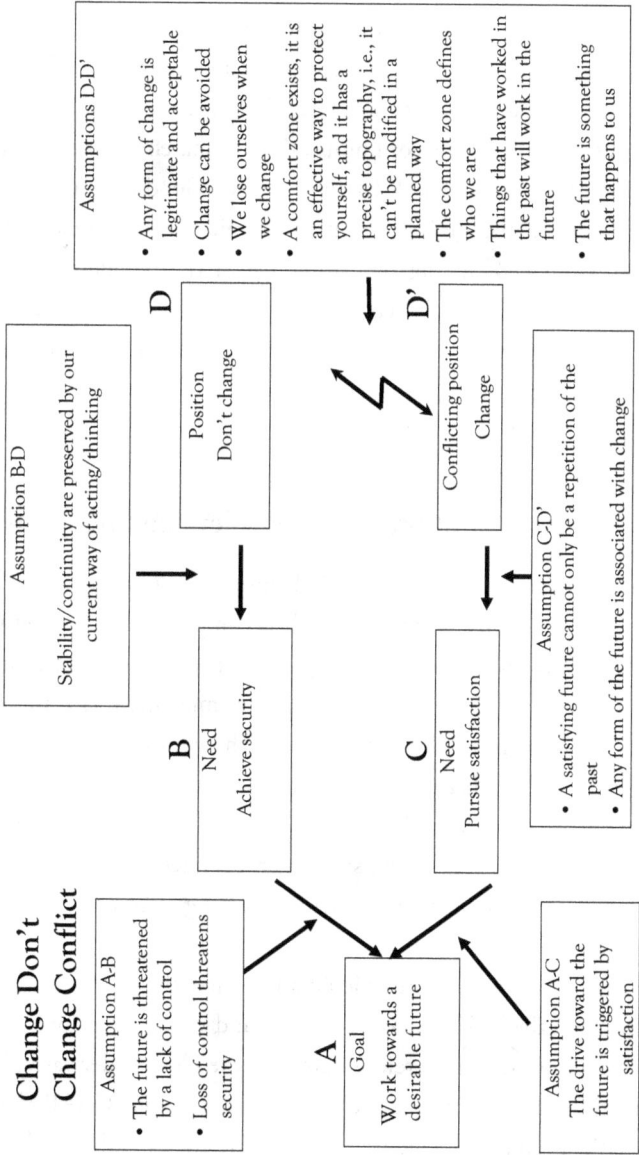

Figure 8.1 The Change vs. Don't Change conflict

to be exercised on the "pieces" that make up their organization. Their rationale is: *If I control the individual pieces, I will have a handle on the whole.* Legions of Comptrollers are hired precisely for that reason and, still today, the core teachings of Business Schools revolve around the dogma of accounting for costs and the quest for their "rational allocation." An Accounting Cathedral has been erected to sanctify the Holy Grail of "cost detection and its management," and the whole edifice of "transparency" toward investors in quarterly communications to shareholders rests on the information provided by GAAP-based reporting. Good luck with that.

A shift toward the design of truly systemic organizations that are realistically capable of taking full advantage of the wonders promised by digital and poised to build chains of greater value cannot take place without *rethinking what we want to manage and how we want to measure performances.* Accordingly, even the most primal, rudimentary form of management, "Control," must be reevaluated.

Control and Statistical Understanding

A systemic organization, as we have said before, is a *network of components working together* toward a common goal. The components of this network are the (repetitive) processes and the projects the organization is made of. If we want to "control" the organization, we must then "control" how these processes and projects are performed. The control, to be effective, must be consistent with the nature of the organization; *if* the inherent, defining feature of a system is the interdependence of its components, *then* control must be exercised on such interdependencies.

This is precisely where conventional accounting stops providing valuable input and begins to be misleading.

Accounting was invented in Medici's Florence; the double entry system is, in fact, called "The Italian Method" and was devised long before calculus came about. It is therefore devoid of the idea of "derivative" and consequently lacks the concepts of speed and motion. GAAP, despite the acrobatic attempts of patching up its deficiencies with "Cash Flow Statements" and all the forms of measuring money inflow (e.g., EBITDA), remains a fairly archaic, static, (pre)-Newtonian way of measuring performances. Most certainly, it is inadequate to support decision making in environments where speed of Flow is paramount.

So, if "controlling the pieces," the game of conventional accounting, is inadequate and hinders the transformation from silo to system, *what do we control and how?*

In previous chapters, I tried to illustrate why variation in processes and their synchronization on a rationally chosen process, called "constraint," are the founding elements for a Deming–Goldratt-based approach to the design and management of organizations. The Decalogue methodology was developed to support that design (that we called "Systemic Organization Cartoon"). How do we transform that Cartoon *operationally* into a living and breathing organization and how do we manage it?

Remember, management is about prediction, what we can anticipate as the outcome for an action we intend to take. Placing emphasis on Predictive Statistical Studies, originally developed by Walter Shewhart, in the management of organizations was the hallmark of Dr. Deming's teachings. This is precisely what we need to do: *understand how variation affects the flow of all the main processes making up the system.* A very comprehensive body of knowledge has been developed for this purpose and it goes under the name of Statistical Process Control (SPC). Over the last 25 years, I witnessed firsthand the wealth of knowledge it brings to the life of companies in every sector.

SPC does not just provide a nondeterministic understanding of numbers; unlike the "seat of the pants" variance analysis of traditional budgeting activities, SPC provides insight into the *predictability* of processes. It allows a rigorous evaluation of the intrinsic level of reliability with which processes are operated and, most importantly, provides the focus necessary to launch improvement process initiatives. Simply put, *there can be no sustainable improvement, let alone effective control, without statistical insight.*

The applications of SPC in organizations are limited only by the imagination of managers.

SPC shows how different work methods, behaviors, market situations, and equipment interplay to generate an outcome; it provides invaluable understanding of how one critical variable under observation is evolving in time and informs the thinking associated with controlling and improving that variable (e.g., the variation affecting the consumption of project buffers). If leaders and managers are serious about "control," they must embrace the idea of *statistical understanding* of the phenomena they want to exert control over and set up a way to measure it. In the Appendix, we provide information about how systemic measurements can be made.

Control and Constraint in Projects

How do we go about exerting control over projects, the lifeblood of a successful organization?

Dr. Goldratt tackles the issue of variation from a different angle. He looks at the "cumulated variation" generated in the system (we can call it "covariance") and where it could produce the most damage, on the constraint. Instead of looking at the variation of individual processes, the Theory of Constraints leverages statistical understanding of the properties of cumulated variations to establish a "buffer" to protect the constraint. Most importantly, the buffer, if managed, provides insight into the inner workings of *the system as a whole*. We can look at the buffer as an "oscillator"; as such, it can be understood in terms of its variation, just like any process in the organization.

A project is a collection of interrelated activities aimed at achieving a goal within a given timeframe and specified parameters (typically, money and specs). These activities must be orchestrated through tasks that follow some logical sequence, and part of that logic is the availability of the resources needed to perform the tasks. Moreover, each resource (humans, but also machines) has different skills (competencies) and although not all of them are of the same level, they can all be useful for the completion of the multitude of projects that make up the organization.

In a project, the *constraint* is the longest chain of dependent events (tasks) that takes into account the availability of resources/competencies (the ones that must execute the tasks). A "realistic" way to manage a project, one that can anticipate its outcome in terms of specs, timeline, and budget, must take into account the *finiteness* of resources. For this reason, Dr. Goldratt described this arrangement of resources on a timeline as "finite capacity scheduling" and called it *Critical Chain*, in order to distinguish it from the more popular (and misleading) Critical Path.

The Critical Chain algorithm for managing projects leverages well-known statistical features of cumulated variation to establish a buffer at the end of the Critical Chain (the "Constraint" of the project). This project buffer will contract or expand based on its consumption (tasks can be completed early as well as late): *if* buffer oscillation measured with SPC techniques (called Control Charts) shows statistical predictability *and* the range of this oscillation is smaller than the length of the buffer, *then* the project has a high probability of finishing on time. Most importantly, if the Control Chart exhibits lack of statistical predictability, we will have very early warnings that something is going wrong and we can intervene. Using SPC to monitor the consumption of Project Buffers is an innovation of the Decalogue methodology and provides a more scientifically rigorous and insightful way to manage the overall project than dividing the project buffer into zones. (See the Appendix for further information on Control Charts.)

The Critical Chain Method for managing projects was devised to accelerate the development of new products; its stomping ground was R&D. Indeed, it can be used to manage any project and I have been personally involved in several implementations and in many different environments, from Industry to M&A.

Invariably, the main obstacle to reaping the benefit of the Critical Chain approach has been the availability of resources due to an organizational design that was siloed. *If* we look at the pool of available resources/competencies as belonging to different silos *and* the performance of the individual silos are measured, by definition, individually, *then* there will always be reluctance from the Head of the silo to allow "their" resources to be used in a "cross-silo" project. "Teamwork," and all the training on how to do it best, in the end, becomes just a feel-good, nice word developed by HR to justify the work of their silo.

What my colleagues and I began to see, with greater and greater clarity, starting from the early 2000s, is that the Critical Chain algorithm can be *the harbinger for a new organizational design.*

If an organization is, essentially, an ongoing collection of unfolding projects, then the focus of leadership (Board, C-Suite, etc.) *must be* on how well and timely these projects are executed. The "Control" must be exercised where projects going haywire would produce real damage: on the Constraint, indeed.

Hence, any form of meaningful control can only be exercised through managing the Buffer that is the real thermometer that measures the temperature of the organization.

By constantly monitoring the state of the buffer for each of the ongoing projects, leadership can have a real insight, *not* numbers from a spreadsheet, into how well the flow of events is generating units of the goal the organization is pursuing.

Unlocking the Potential of Everyone in the Organization

The Transformation from Silo to System is fueled by the Critical Chain algorithm developed by Dr. Goldratt and sustained by relentless attention to the management of variation throughout the system. We shall talk about the cognitive shift needed to operate that shift in Chapter 10.

A critical aspect of this organizational transformation is the way human potential and value is unlocked. Each individual has talents, drive, inventiveness, and many other characteristics that make him/her unique; each of these must be leveraged. One of the most critical is his/her *competencies*, the skills and the aptitudes he/she is capable of contributing.

All of us are capable of doing different things, have different skills, and have personal traits; in a siloed organization, our competencies are straight-jacketed into what the silo needs in order to enhance its locally measured performance. In a project-based organizational structure, each and every one of these talents is leveraged to maximize its contribution to the overall performance and to increase the number of projects that can be successfully run simultaneously.

Not every competence that any individual possesses is of the same level; Ms. Smith may be capable of performing, say, five different kinds of activities but not necessarily all at the same level. Let's say that she can perform A and B with great dexterity, whereas C and D with a good (not great) skill; but she is also capable of contributing a modest amount of competence in activities such as D.

If an organization is running in parallel a multitude of projects, the more it can deploy suitable *competencies*, the more it has a chance to complete these projects successfully. And so, it may well be that a modest amount of competence in activity D is what it takes in project X to finish on time without having to wait for somebody with a higher level of skill D but who is busy performing on a task in another project. Ms. Smith's modest amount of competence in D (in a project with tasks that require only a modest amount of the D competence) could be all that is needed to finish on time.

In a "system," as opposed to a "silo" organization, the name of the game is how well I can leverage what I've got for a global result. A project-based organization epitomizes, algorithmically, exactly this concept.

In a project-based organization, we can finally make sense of the all too vague idea of "Teamwork"; we can actually have people working in Teams without resorting to excruciating and hilariously off-putting "team-building" sessions. We can simply facilitate teamwork by *removing the barriers that prevent it*; we can do so by orchestrating people's talents and skills in a time-sensitive and continuously evolving Network of Projects, bearing in mind the overall goal of the organization, whether financial or otherwise.

The guiding scheduling principle to build successful Networks of Critically Chained projects is, then, the availability of *Competencies* that each Resource brings to the table.

Silos are a sickness that can be cured. In the end, ignorance (on how to do it) is a condition that can be addressed; stupidity (refusing to learn it) is a choice. As Dr. Deming would put it: "Learning is not compulsory, but neither is survival."

Curing the Silo Sickness: Let's Sum It Up

1. A functional structure is not suitable to support the systemic approach to managing organizations in our new digital age. Organizations, by the nature of their work, are cooperative and cross-functional. This is because *none of the activities of any company can be performed within the narrow boundaries of a single function.*

2. Any plausible template for an organizational structure that can foster cooperative work must also take into account the evolution in time of the interdependencies needed to accomplish any activity.

3. In essence, the management of any organization becomes the management of a network of recurring, orderly, and evolving-in-time activities. We call them projects. Control is exercised through ensuring orderly coordination, not functional reporting.

4. The backbone of any organizational effort becomes, then, the ability to manage the *network of projects* that comprises any organization.

5. The springboard to overcome the paradigm of today's functional silo structure is the idea of a company seen as a network (with a stated goal) of projects.

How to Build the New Organization for the Digital Age: Principles, Methods, and Tools

How can we do this on a practical level? By combining the approach of the Theory of Constraints with a purely systemic view based on interdependencies and interactions.

In other words, we do so by

1. Building interdependent processes managed through the control of *variation*

2. Subordinating these interdependencies to a strategically chosen element of the system called "*constraint*"

3. Designing the organization as a *network of interdependent projects* with a goal

It's time we stopped repeating the mistakes of the past and embraced our new reality of complexity. As former Navy Seal Chris Fussell concludes in his article, "The battlefield experience that made me realize the danger of silos and isolated teams," *I realized just how far we had to go. There was no single person who bureaucratically owned this issue, no stand-alone order that would force us to collaborate. This would be a culture change, something that would take years …*

If we no longer have silos that we can control vertically as "parts," what we can control are the buffers of projects managed at finite capacity with Critical Chain. These buffers provide protection for ongoing projects and the buffers can be monitored using SPC. It would even be possible to create a kind of "dashboard" that would give leaders real-time information on exactly what is happening in the projects that make up the work of the organization. To this end, we have developed an algorithm (and a piece of technology out of it) that we call Ess3ntial (www.ess3ntial.com).

We live in a digital world that is transforming. We work, increasingly, in a network of networks. We have the science, and thanks to the contribution of two major management thinkers, Dr. W. Edwards Deming and Dr. Eliyahu Goldratt, we also have the method and the tools. Let's put them to work.

Summary of Chapter 8

- Control and vision are two fundamental needs that must be satisfied for individuals and organizations.
- Decision making involves us in the dilemma Change *vs.* Don't Change.
- Traditional hierarchies satisfy the need to control based on the assumption that it is possible to exert control over the whole organization by controlling the "pieces" of the organization, and accounting methods are based on this assumption.
- Designing an organization that takes full advantage of digital technology and building chains of greater value cannot take place without rethinking what we want to manage and how we want to measure performances.
- A systemic organization takes into account interdependencies, and traditional accounting is inadequate and misleading as it cannot support decision making where speed of flow is paramount.
- To manage and control an organization, we must understand how variation affects the flow of all the main processes making up the system, and SPC serves this purpose.
- If leaders and managers are serious about "control," they must embrace the idea of *statistical understanding* of the phenomena they want to exert control over and set up a way to measure it.
- To be completed within budget and on time, Projects must be managed taking into account finite resources.
- Using the Critical Chain Project Management method based on finite capacity scheduling, we can protect projects with a buffer at the end that expands and contracts based on its consumption. This consumption can be monitored statistically using SPC.

- Silos interfere with the availability of resources.
- Critical Chain can become the engine for a systemic organization design.
- By constantly monitoring the state of the buffer for each of the ongoing projects, leadership can have a real insight into how well the flow of events is generating units of the goal the organization is pursuing.
- Projects require varying levels of competencies.
- We can unlock the potential of individuals in organizations by building a network of synchronized projects based on scheduling competencies.
- The principles, methods, and tools to work within a network of networks already exist. See www.ess3ntial.com.

What Comes Next

The following chapter is written by Stefano Righetti, CEO of Hyphen-Italia, from the point of view of an entrepreneur who has embraced the systemic model I have put forward in this book. The idea of a systemic organization is something we began to discuss many years ago when Stefano first took an interest in a Deming and Goldratt approach to management. By working together, Stefano absorbed and built on the concept of the organization as a system. He saw the need to conceive the software products Hyphen produces in a logic of flow and has persevered in communicating to clients a systemic view of the work of organizations as fundamental for success with digitization. Thanks to Stefano, Intelligent Management has gained understanding of the intricacies of developing and implementing digital technologies and the systemic implications. Stefano's chapter describes his personal journey with digital technology and his insight and experience add significantly to the message of this book.

CHAPTER 9

Interweaving the Product Supply Chain with the Digital Supply Chain to Improve Business Performance and Competitiveness

Stefano Righetti, CEO Hyphen-Italia

As a Founder of Hyphen, my experience with digital technology began with providing software solutions for the publishing world. We have evolved to become an international leader in assisting top fashion and luxury brands and retailers through their digital journey.

Digital Transformation is an expression that we see everywhere, but what does it really mean? There are many different points of view on this and the situation is constantly evolving; however, as the name suggests, introducing the digital dimension into any organization does not just mean making changes. It is a major shift. It does not simply involve introducing new technology; it calls for a radical rethinking of how we do business and how our organizations function and are shaped. Digital Transformation is no longer an option but a necessity for businesses of any size and level of complexity. It is the only way to remain competitive in a world that switches ever more rapidly between old and new ways of communicating and where omnichannel sales are key.

However, when it comes to taking action, it often becomes evident that there is a lack of clarity about what it entails. It is not simply a matter of adopting new technologies or shifting to the cloud. First and foremost, Digital Transformation is a *change in company culture* and involves a new understanding of how the organization must work. Digital calls for remodeling processes and information flows and adopting new business models fit to exploit the opportunities ushered in by new technologies, new media, and new communication channels. Digital technologies can help to support and manage processes. They can broaden and orient the *network of conversations* among the people involved. The tools and services that technologies offer can help to govern the hyperconnectivity that comes with a digital world so that it improves the quality of people's lives and the company's business performance.

The only way to absorb such a radical level of change is to adopt a robust approach, a rigorous method, and adequate tools. This requires both long- and short-term strategies made up of intermediate steps so that the organization can become fully digital without stumbling along the way.

For example, by introducing e-commerce or entering the most frequented marketplaces (Amazon, etc.), a business will not automatically achieve higher sales and improved performance. What is required, instead, is a complete rethinking of the processes and business model with which the company does business. This rethinking must start with a thorough analysis of the current reality, followed by a consistent redesign of processes that will impact various aspects of the digital supply chain of a product. Only in this way will a company reap all the benefits of these extraordinary new digital means that would be impossible without the right amount of preparation.

The Essence of Digital Transformation: New Synergies Between the Product Supply Chain and the Digital Supply Chain

Over the last 15 years, our work with top fashion, luxury brands, and retailers has taught us that there can be no real digital transformation unless it *starts from the production flow of digital content of products and the brand,* also known as the product editorial process. It is this content that provides the fuel that feeds the transformation process, and companies need to create the right structure to produce this content with the right workflows and digital tools.

Unfortunately, more often than not, what happens is that the creation of digital content for a product and a brand is handed over to people working in the Digital Supply Chain, to those involved in designing, producing, and distributing editorial material for communication for omnichannel promotion and sales activities. In reality, it is wrong to think that the Digital Supply Chain people are the only ones in possession of the assets, data, and information connected with products. Indeed, they often have a hard time searching within their own organization to find product content created months earlier, during the first phases of the product life cycle.

This happens because, within the life cycle of a product, various people at different levels contribute to producing assets and information about the product, and this process is often underestimated and overlooked. In every organization, there are content generators and content consumers. A thorough review and redesign of the processes connected with the production and sharing of product content is where an effective transformation process must start.

Digital is radically changing *how and where* brands reach out to consumers. Interactions between brands and consumers are now happening at a speed and in ways that were previously inconceivable and the number of channels and media where brands need to be present has greatly multiplied. While it is true that this new, multichannel reality is creating new opportunities for building relationships, it is also causing unprecedented organizational complexity that is disrupting traditional business models.

The new paradigms for multichannel communication, promotion, and sales are forcing brands to build a solid *Digital Supply Chain*. However, the processes for producing and using digital content often lack alignment and synchronization with the operational needs of the people involved in the *Product Supply Chain*. For example, samples may not be produced in a timely fashion for e-commerce photos. Whenever a company produces content for the editorial process of a product, there must always be timely contact with the product supply chain. The two supply chains, digital and physical, must intertwine like the strands of DNA with the right pace and synchronization.

For this reason, embarking on the path of digitization, as we stated, inevitably involves tackling an organizational redesign, and this endeavor must be supported by a suitable method and adequate tools.

As illustrated in Figure 9.1, in our opinion, there can be no real digital transformation unless the Product Supply Chain is synchronized with the Digital Supply Chain. The Product Supply Chain and the Digital Supply Chain must intertwine and interdepend and this connection must be supported by an adequate organizational design and tools that help us manage the inevitable entropy.

Let me emphasize that again: Digitization is no longer a choice. The more an organization is capable of operating the digital shift proficiently, the more competitive it will become. The opposite is sadly true and there are already casualties among brands who have not been able to make the shift in time.

One more time: successful digital transformation can only take place when the digital content supply chain is integrated effectively with the product supply chain.

There are at least six main areas, or layers, where this change has to happen (Figure 9.2):

1. Sales
2. Communication and Promotion
3. Product R&D
4. Industrial Processes
5. Logistics
6. Management of work environment (Comfort, Productivity, Safety, Sustainability)

Our work over the last 15 years has been primarily in the areas of Sales, Communication and Promotion, and product R&D. An integral part of this work is about producing the Digital Product (and brand) Identity that is necessary to represent the product on the web.

Déjà vu from the Publishing Industry

Having worked with traditional publishing, I realized something: a transformation process had already occurred "behind the scenes." The printing

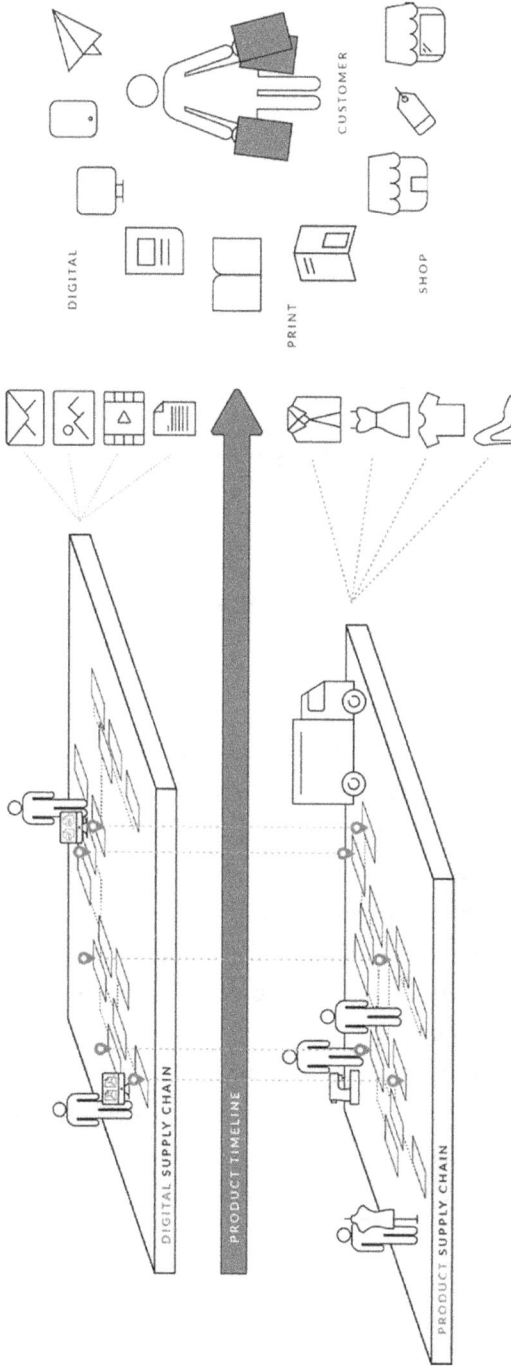

Figure 9.1 Interdependence between the Product Supply Chain and the Digital Supply Chain

Source: Courtesy of Hyphen Library.

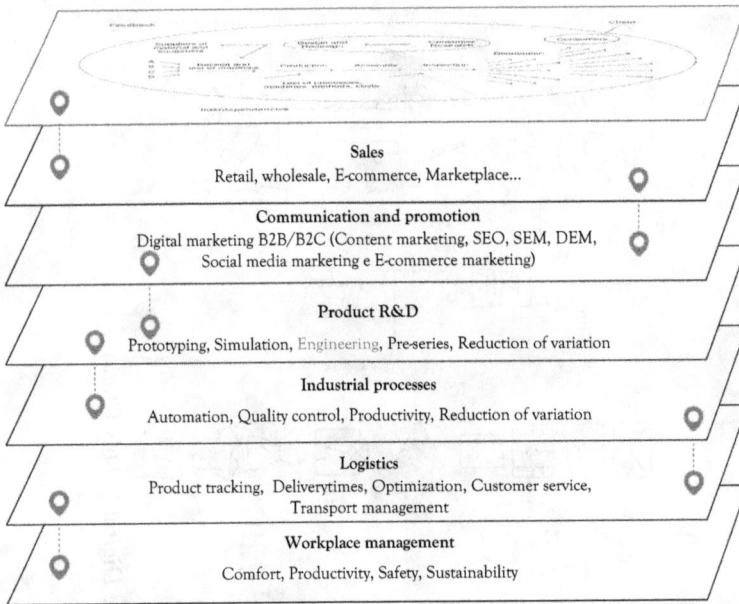

Figure 9.2 The six layers of digital transformation
Source: Courtesy of Hyphen Library.

process shifted from physical to digital, but this was not noticed by consumers at large—all they saw was a proliferation of new products available, but for those working in the sector it was nothing short of a revolution. When Apple introduced Desktop publishing in the early 1990s, everything changed.

The Digital Revolution that occurred in the publishing world did not only change the process of printing; digital technology impacted every process involved, from the concept of a magazine, book, flyer, to the production of finished materials. Desktop publishing revolutionized the techniques for the creation, prepress preparation, and printing of published products. Just a few years later, print was no longer the only channel for publishing and soon became secondary compared to digital publishing and the web.

What unites the transformation that took place within traditional publishing and the new digital transformation is *content*! The editorial process was the "factory" for the printing trade. Omnichannel communication is leading companies to understand that content (editorial material) is increasingly important for them. We began to propose to our brand customers the same change process that we had provided to large publishers: *Brands become actual publishers.*

Brands and Retailers Are Publishers

Digital technology is removing the distance, physical and otherwise, between communication, promotion, and purchasing. Until not so long ago, our need or desire for a product or service led us to look for them in physical stores so we could get to know them and develop an interest that could then convert into a sale. Today, our desire for products is stimulated through direct or indirect digital forms of communication. We can look, assess, and purchase through the same media without any mediation or interruption in terms of time or logistics. This means there is a strong "emotional" factor in purchasing as there is no longer the same time lapse that allows consumers to plan or change their minds.

The editorial content associated with the brand and its products is what becomes the primary element in communication and promotion. It is what allows communication to take place. Without quality (and self-explanatory) content, the whole process of communication, promotion, and sales comes to a halt.

In every digital project, it is imperative to know what can be the starting point for the creation of editorial content. Also, many projects fail for lack of digital content or because the cost of that content is too high; digital connection with customers requires timeliness and availability of high-quality content. In order to have good digital content, companies must start the process of creating that content right from the start. Indeed, it is becoming increasingly important to have a digital rendering of a product before it goes into production. This is no longer just an R&D concern; Marketing must be able to test the product and so its digital version is now essential.

In essence:

- Products (and services) now need a digital version that represents them on the web (i.e., the touch-points where the product/service is shown, communicated, and sold) and this has to take into account who will be seeing this version, what their needs are, which permissions are required, and which devices are used.
- This is not only relevant for the B2C world. The digital version of a product is the "passport" that is required

throughout its lifetime and all through the value chain, from conception through to customer service, as well as for all the various phases of communication, promotion, and sales.

The Digital Identity of Products and Brands

Product Digital Identity (PDI) is a leverage point, a key factor in the journey of a company toward its digital transformation (Figure 9.3). It is its "passport" in the omnichannel universe. PDI encompasses all the content that is used to represent the product in the digital world; this content is determined by what a channel/device is authorized to publish and typically consists of images, video, designs, 3D, tests, characteristics, tags, links, filters, and so on.

Creating PDI and managing it within a company in the most standardized, "industrial" way possible can be an important catalyst for the digital transformation journey. Ideally, PDI should be coupled with an organizational approach that is "systemic" and consistent with the project-like nature of the work being carried out. Enabling a management system based on this "network of projects" in my opinion (and experience) will certainly boost the process of digitization.

In summary, PDI is key because of the following:

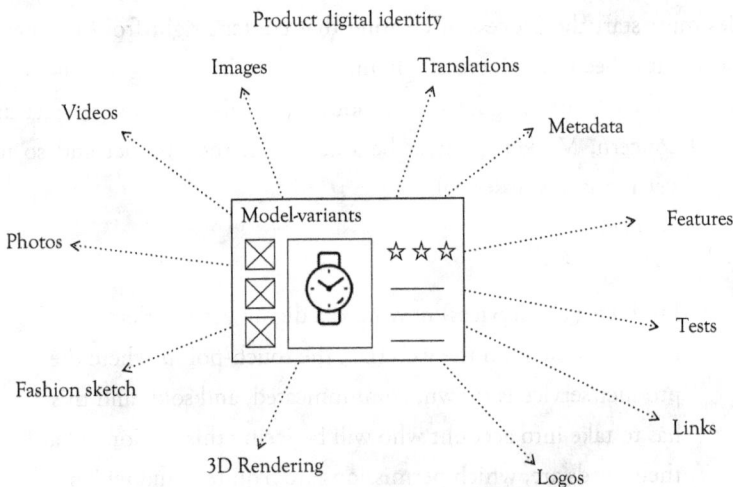

Figure 9.3 Product Digital Identity (PDI)
Source: Courtesy of Hyphen Library.

1. The PDI is crucial during the distribution of assets to various channels as it provides a means of connecting all the text and interactive content that represent the product on the web. For this purpose, it is not sufficient to have a set of images with metadata; what is needed is a new digital entity that represents the product in its entirety, bringing together in one location the technical characteristics of the product/service, its attributes, history, images and video, and in general, all its multimedia and interactive elements.

2. PDI is becoming increasingly part of the business and service that supports the relationship with retail and wholesale.

3. Brands must be able to deliver their products in a digital version to those who communicate it to the market, possibly before they are delivered physically to shop shelves. Customers will want to see a new iPhone before it becomes available in the Apple Stores.

4. Brands must consider the process of generating the digital version of a product in the same way that they think of the physical production process and do so in a highly standardized, "industrial" way.

5. The digital version of a product is essential for selling products through Retailers and Wholesalers. The information that is supplied to the consumer and that sales staff use to explain the product to customers comes from the same systems that manage the PDI.

The Digital Editorial Process of a Product

Brands are drowning in the vast and varied content that comes with each product. Brands struggle to locate product content or even know who is the right person that has such information. Furthermore, they often discover that other people and departments have also been producing and using the same assets and this means unnecessary duplication of work. The existence of silos only exacerbates these time-consuming redundancies, and the more products there are, the greater the confusion that is created.

We realized that what was required was a *systemic* solution to help organizations along the path of digital transformation. We identified three pillars to make the solution work:

Pillar 1: Product Digital Identity (PDI)

This is where we create a mapping between a product and its digital identity. Every product or project will build up a digital "passport." Various elements from different roles and sources will contribute material to this digital passport, such as sketches, texts, tags, video, 3D, images, copy, and translations.

Pillar 2: Product Editorial Process

Every department or role in a company is a content producer and designs, creates, and adapts a single product identity, often at the same time. Without an underlying infrastructure to support work-flows, content can get lost, inconsistencies can be created, and local archiving can prevent access. For this reason, we developed a Product Editorial Process to automate, optimize, and support each company's distinct internal workflows (Figure 9.4).

Pillar 3: Digital Library

How do we store and access all of the content? We came to the conclusion that what is required is a Digital Library. This is a technological tool to catalogue, tag, and adapt content for different purposes. It provides a structure to hold this all together. Instead of chaos, digital assets can be managed through a Digital Library to save time, increase productivity, and support creativity. Indeed, no

Digital content as raw material to nourish the market

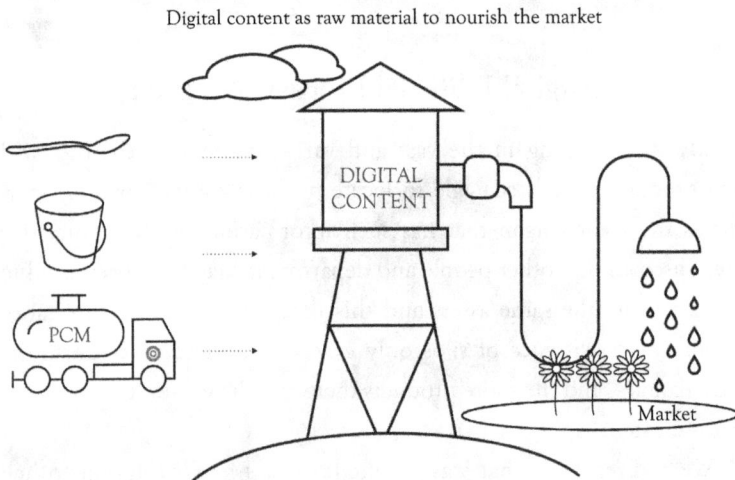

Figure 9.4 Digital content as raw material

Source: Courtesy of Hyphen Library.

Figure 9.5 Digital Library
Source: Courtesy of Hyphen Library.

front-end/front-store service or application can be successful if the company does not have quality digital content that can be accessed in a timely way (Figure 9.5).

Online Business Versus Offline Business

Many people believe that the very existence of the Retail/Wholesale world is threatened by online business. In reality, the problem is that current commercial and distribution models are not always compatible with what is now happening in the market because of digital. Today, there are ways of engaging customers, communicating and promoting products through digital media and devices; these new ways are aligned with new pathways in the "Customer Journey" and can disrupt current commercial and distribution models.

A functional hierarchy and the budget-inspired, local optimum-driven decision making it brings with it can seriously hinder the creation of digital ways of establishing relationships and selling.

Any nonsystemic behaviors create internal conflicts that will, directly or indirectly, generate suboptimal communication with the customer to the benefit of the competition. Unfortunately, only a few organizations are able to compete with "digital native" retail giants who are inherently able to satisfy (and introduce) the new customer journey and purchasing models in a truly omnichannel way. There are brands, for instance, for whom it is irrelevant if a consumer goes to a physical store and then buys online or vice versa. There must of course be consistency between the selection of goods seen online and what is displayed in the stores as well as the way in which products are displayed and represented online and offline.

A fundamental element of the "Customer Journey" is the User Experience of the consumer during their journey, and an essential part of this experience is created by the editorial content for the product and brand. The quality, depth, and availability of this content will increasingly influence the choices of the consumer and the relationship with them and, consequently, determine the business performance of a company.

Producing Content

There is often mention of the idea of a Content Factory as a way of producing and managing digital content and materials. I believe that a Content Factory must belong to the brand with the goal of creating and managing the digital editorial process end to end. It must be supported by new tools and services that can enhance performance and automation and should be as independent as possible from the destination/channel where the content will be used. More in general, my idea of a Content Factory is an operational model supported by adequate tools/services that can direct the network of conversations of all those involved in producing, managing, and distributing product, editorial, and brand content while keeping control and ownership of the brand assets.

In order to create a valuable Content Factory, companies can adopt workflow models that have been used for some time in the publishing world by updating them with a new approach and methods and adequate e-business services. What is needed is a network for common use of content that can be internal or external. It requires new competencies to oversee this process and a different mindset.

One of the (many) dilemmas that every brand faces in trying to gain control of the end-to-end digital editorial process is the one connected with the creation of digital assets in the form of photographic images. Understanding the fundamental assumptions upon which this conflict rests allows for the development of a tailor-made transformation plan that can be designed and controlled all through its execution. The conflict cloud we have included here is an example developed with a world famous luxury fashion brand we have worked with for many years. Yet again, the solution, although heavily supported by technology, has been the result of a shift in understanding of the role that a systemic organization should play in embracing digitization and the strategic, organizational, and operational changes that this understanding implies (Figures 9.6 and 9.7).

The Role of the Digital Supply Chain in Business Performance

In a world where the relationship of the customer with a product and brand essentially begins and is managed through digital channels and media, the Digital Supply Chain plays a primary business role. It is not an exaggeration to say that the editorial process of a product (and/or Brand) is becoming equivalent to the product supply chain. Indeed, in some cases, the digital version of the product is more important than the physical production.

The quality and completeness of content have become major means of conversion in retail and it is a revolution that is affecting all sectors. Digital content enriches the product and when the shop window is digital, photography plays a crucial role. As we like to say in Hyphen, "no photo, no business." For this reason, we were able to develop our HSL (Hyphen Still Life) technology that renders the photographic process highly standardized and "industrial." In this way, photography does not become a "bottleneck" in the digitization process.

When Gutenberg invented the printing press, he essentially created a container of content and now that container has become digital. Today, digital is no longer an option—to paraphrase Descartes, "I am digital therefore I am." However, we have to pay attention to the *quality* of the digital production line and there has to be synchronization between the digital and physical supply chains. This involves a network of conversations among the various roles involved. We need a "digital quality system" and we can look to the work of W. Edwards Deming for inspiration. By adopting the kind of systemic organization design that Deming introduced, along with accurate process mapping/design and control charts, the industrial and digital processes can work in parallel.

Here are some major considerations regarding improving business performance through Digital Transformation:

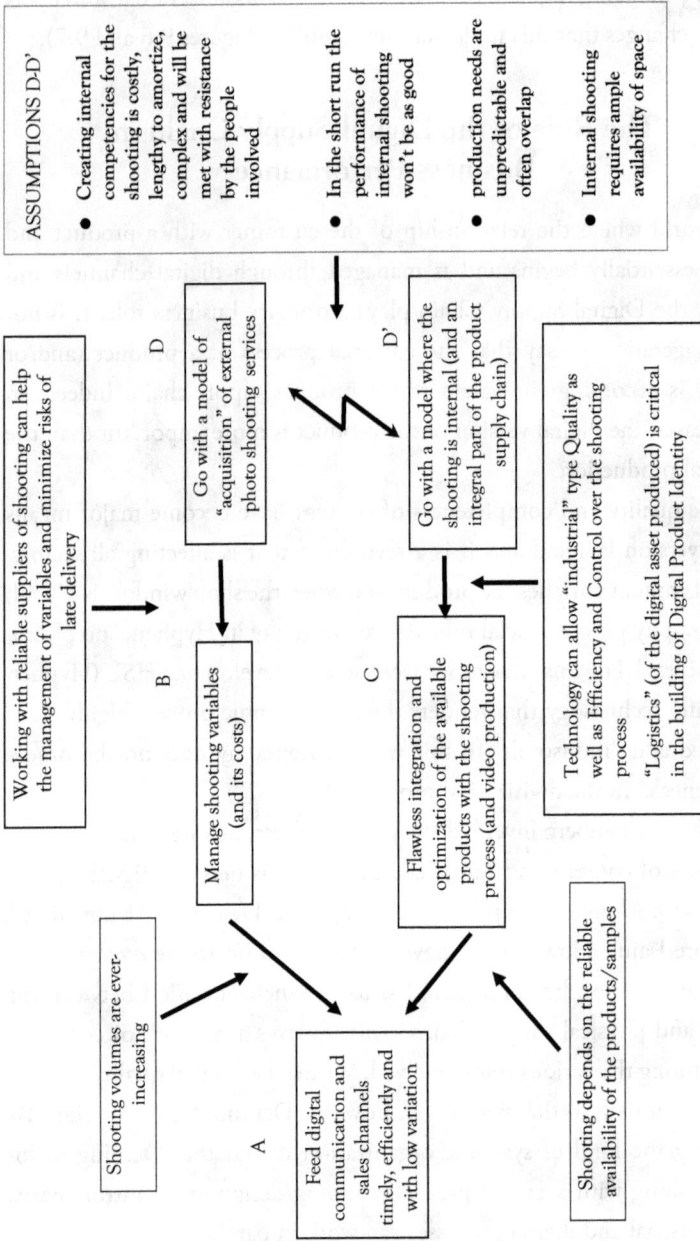

Figure 9.6 Product photography conflict

Source: Courtesy of Hyphen Library.

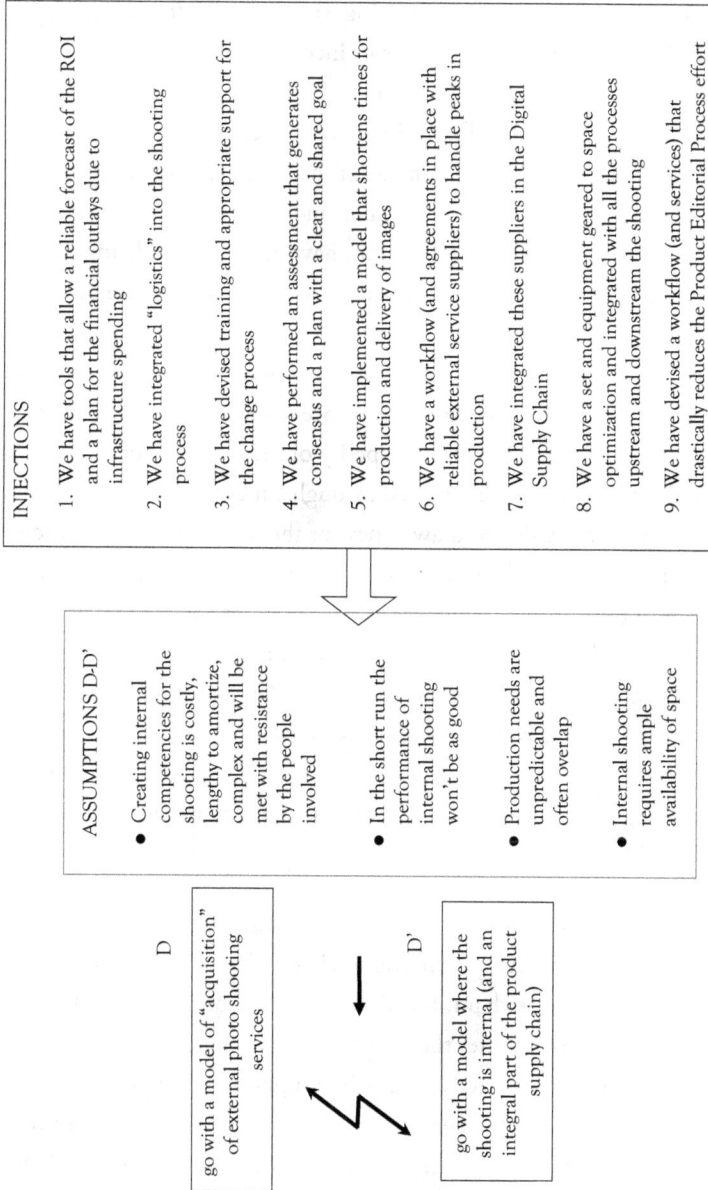

Figure 9.7 Product photography conflict continued

Source: Courtesy of Hyphen Library.

INJECTIONS

1. We have tools that allow a reliable forecast of the ROI and a plan for the financial outlays due to infrastructure spending

2. We have integrated "logistics" into the shooting process

3. We have devised training and appropriate support for the change process

4. We have performed an assessment that generates consensus and a plan with a clear and shared goal

5. We have implemented a model that shortens times for production and delivery of images

6. We have a workflow (and agreements in place with reliable external service suppliers) to handle peaks in production

7. We have integrated these suppliers in the Digital Supply Chain

8. We have a set and equipment geared to space optimization and integrated with all the processes upstream and downstream the shooting

9. We have devised a workflow (and services) that drastically reduces the Product Editorial Process effort

ASSUMPTIONS D-D'

• Creating internal competencies for the shooting is costly, lengthy to amortize, complex and will be met with resistance by the people involved

• In the short run the performance of internal shooting won't be as good

• Production needs are unpredictable and often overlap

• Internal shooting requires ample availability of space

D

go with a model of "acquisition" of external photo shooting services

D'

go with a model where the shooting is internal (and an integral part of the product supply chain)

1. The editorial process of a product is taking on the same level of importance as the physical production of the product itself. Without digital content (Digital Identity of a Product) the product cannot be presented in a complete and winning way along the digital highways, it will provide the user with little or incorrect information, sales will diminish, and inventory will increase. In other words, the economic/financial performance of a business will depend increasingly on the availability, quality, and alignment of the digital content of products and brands, regardless of the business model or type of market.

2. Product content, specifically photos, have evolved from being a support element for communication and promotion to become business processes.

3. Digital transformation is no longer an option for businesses. The level of digitization of company processes will be a determining element for the survival and prosperity of the organization.

4. Synchronization can be achieved through a method and actions that enable understanding and awareness of the organization as a whole system made up of the processes and micro processes that constitute and feed the product supply chain. This requires a logistics that integrates digital with the product supply chain.

5. A true digital transformation can only take place when the Digital Supply Chain is integrated and is in harmony with the Product Supply Chain.

6. Involving suppliers is fundamental for transforming them into "Digital Partners."

Indeed, a critical element is also the integration of the Digital Supply Chain with the entire ecosystem (value chain) that supports any business. This is not a linear chain, but rather a system of interacting nodes, each one of which contributes their own version of digital content. These nodes need to be synchronized and possibly supported by a platform that allows them to operate in synergy to avoid redundancies. This is something that businesses have been trying to achieve for some time and there are various obstacles, including technological ones. However, I have come to believe that they all boil down to the way organizations are designed and managed.

Digital Transformation Requires a Systemic Approach

One of the greatest challenges of digital transformation is the overwhelming complexity involved. How is it possible to deal with the multiplicity of organizational roles and processes that must be included in the transformation? Where do you start?

Successful digital transformation must start from a unifying vision, something that lends structure and sense to a seemingly endless task. However, the way to create unity is not simply to attempt to tie the various "fragments" of an organization together. The recipe cannot be "divide and conquer." It has to be much more fundamental and radical to be adequate for our age of complexity. This is something that W. Edwards Deming taught us long ago. Undoubtedly, there are costs involved in the transformation process and many companies measure these costs only in terms of marketing.

What is missing is an understanding of the costs incurred by the entropy that arises from *not* synchronizing the physical and digital product supply chains and the difficulties involved in building this parallel relationship.

In summary, Digital Transformation means

- Supporting and managing processes using Digital Technologies
- Broadening, directing, and managing the network of conversations among people involved in the various roles and the tools/services based on digital technologies
- Governing the hyper-connectivity offered by the digital world, using it to serve people and improve their quality of life, and to improve the business performance of the organization
- Integrating, harmonizing, and synchronizing the Digital Supply Chain with the Product Supply Chain
- Designing and managing a company as a whole system to facilitate and accelerate flow and to direct the network of conversations in the direction of achieving the goal of the organization

CHAPTER 10

Changing How We Think for the Digital Age

Domenico Lepore, Angela Montgomery, and Giovanni Siepe

Everyone doing his best is not the answer. It is first necessary that people know what to do. Drastic changes are required. The first step in the transformation is to learn how to change ... Long-term commitment to new learning and new philosophy is required of any management that seeks transformation. The timid and the fainthearted, and people that expect quick results, are doomed to disappointment.

—W. Edwards Deming

Every single thing that happens in a company, from how strategy is designed to how a widget or a software is made and sold, is the *end result* of one specific human activity: thinking. In many companies, the thinking that originates the actions that follow is, at best, vague. Anyone who has sat in enough meetings knows this.

Why is so much thinking in organizations vague? It's not because people lack intelligence or qualifications. The fact is that the kind of thinking that can produce high-quality results at a *systemic* level needs to be learned, but who is teaching it?

Dr. Eliyahu Goldratt declared that his mission was to "teach the world to think." At Intelligent Management, we have had the privilege of sharing the Thinking Processes developed by Goldratt with dozens of companies over the years. What is perhaps most exciting is to see how these Thinking Processes raise the *collective intelligence* in any organization. They allow people to achieve real focus *together, as a group*, and then to *act on that focus* in an orderly and effective way. Not only does this work raise collective intelligence, it also leverages the unique intelligence, knowledge, and experience of the group to create breakthroughs and innovation where previously they were stuck.

The faster our world and our markets change through technology, the faster we must acquire systemic thinking skills to think through the shifts and innovations required to lead, adapt, or simply keep up. As we have said, the new covenant that everyone in the organization (as well as the *value chain* in which the organization is embedded) must embrace requires a much higher ability to think, communicate, and act; it requires a new "wiring" in the way we measure, manage, and sustainably improve our efforts toward our goals. Before we take a look at a method for improving our systemic thinking skills, let's look at one of the major obstacles to improving our thinking: an over-reliance on linear thinking.

The Dangers of Too Much Linear Thinking

Linear thinking has served humanity well. Being rational, after all, allowed us to emerge from the dark ages and the realm of superstition. We can thank René Descartes for providing us with a whole system of knowledge and investigation that allowed a description of the world through precise geometric relationships on a plane, including the ability to locate a point by giving its relative distance from perpendicular intersecting lines.

This logic brings us directly to the notion of a matrix. Once again, matrices have allowed us to deepen our understanding of many phenomena. The excel spreadsheet exemplifies the idea of a matrix. The feeling of power and control that tackling problems using a Cartesian approach gives us is incomparable. The problem comes when we try to apply "rational" methods beyond their scope. The Excel spreadsheet is a case in point. It certainly has its merits and is a useful tool for many tasks. However, it becomes an issue when we elevate Excel (or Numbers or any other spreadsheet) to the ranks of a management tool and use it for efforts that require something quite different.

By relying heavily on matrices, we create a dangerously limited view of our reality as organizations. Given the complexity of managing and controlling the combined efforts of many people, it can be tempting to resort to something that gives us the impression of control, such as an organization structured as a matrix. This is linear thinking and it is too limited to encompass the full complexity of human organizations as we understand them today. It leads you to think, erroneously, that if you optimize all the parts the whole will do better. Linear thinking focuses on addressing "symptoms" instead of looking for what is causing the symptoms to happen. In the same way, it leads people to think that individual performance reviews make sense. It fails to recognize that it takes time for a signal to propagate through a system and so the result of an action can only be seen much later, making it harder to understand where the result came from in the first place. It induces us to concentrate on costs and not on how to maximize throughput and it confuses price with value.

Linear thinking imposes old patterns; it expects more of the same because it sees a past that continues in a linear way into the future. For this precise reason, linear thinking is blindsided to disruption. As this book is being written, it is surely not a coincidence that iconic firms have failed under the leadership of CEOs isolated in their office and relying on linear spreadsheets to find out "what was happening" in the business.

We can't keep managing organizations thinking that everything is linear and that a hierarchical functional organization with silos has any chance of being adequate for today's complexity. What we know today that we could not know 50 years ago is that organizations are made up of networks, and they exist within other networks, and all of these networks are made up of multiple interconnections that increase their complexity. The relations within a network evolve in a nonlinear way. Indeed, we may even consider the conflicts that inevitably arise as explosions of nonlinearity. We may state that nonlinearity is the key to interpreting all complex phenomena that arise spontaneously when several entities interact, be they biological or human.

The systemic methodology for management developed by Intelligent Management approaches complexity from a *nonlinear* standpoint. Considerations of network theory led us to develop an organizational model for complexity that we call the Network of Projects described in Chapter 7 to completely shift away from a traditional hierarchical/functional model while protecting the legitimate needs that every organization has for control and growth.

Digitization is accelerating the need to reshape organizations to function beyond silos. Leaders and managers urgently need to get a grasp of knowledge of nonlinearity and learn how to manage organizations in a completely new light. In other words, the evolution that takes us from silos toward a network requires not just a shift in how we organize our work but in *how we think*.

How Can We Boost Our Systemic Intelligence and Learn to Think in a Nonlinear Way?

Learning how to change is perhaps the greatest challenge we face and the most urgent one. Technology demands it and it may not be an exaggeration to say that perhaps our very survival as civilizations depends on it. In this sense, the conflict "Change *vs.* Don't Change" that we saw in Chapter 8 is probably one of the most profound issues of our times. To fully embrace and leverage new technologies to our benefit, we need to learn to think *systemically*. However, this is not usually something that we are taught at school. Indeed, thinking skills in general are not taught, beyond the ability to analyze something logically in terms of grammar or high-school math. Thinking, however, is never a purely logical activity. It is always informed by our emotions, our fears, and our desires. Above all, our thinking is "clouded" by our assumptions and the mental models we inevitably bring with us as part of how our brains have developed. These assumptions and mental models are intimately connected with our personal experiences and the environments where we learned to interact with the world. For example, if we ask an American, a Swede, and a Japanese person what they think about the right for civilians to bear arms, we will no doubt receive very different answers. It is perfectly understandable that people from different backgrounds have different worldviews. However, when people need to interact to achieve a goal, these differing worldviews often lead to conflicts.

The Creative Nature of Conflict

Thanks to the different worldviews or assumptions about reality that various members of any organization or value chain bring to the table, conflict is inevitable. A conflict is a form of "constraint." So far in this book, we have framed several situations or problems as "conflicts" following the approach developed by Dr. Goldratt. The Conflict Cloud is a powerful, structured, and highly effective way to leverage conflict as an opportunity for breakthrough and innovation. Indeed, conflict is an opportunity for creativity.

Why is this so powerful? Because no matter the conflict addressed, it takes into consideration for all parties the two fundamental human drivers: *control* (this connects with fear, restraint, stability, security, immanence, etc.) and *vision* (this connects with desire, expansion, satisfaction, transcendence, etc.). In any conflict, these two needs exist in a variety of manifestations, and any sustainable solution must respect and protect them. This is key to achieving success through conflict.

In our experience at Intelligent Management, every organization has to deal at some level with the most fundamental organizational conflict of adopting a hierarchical structure or not adopting one. How they choose to address this conflict will dictate the pace at which they are able to innovate and grow. The Network of Projects solution was developed as a systemic solution to this fundamental conflict and invalidates many of the assumptions or mental models that keep companies stuck in outmoded models by harmonizing and connecting the work of all those involved. It does so in a way that ensures the needs for vision and control unique to each organization are satisfied.

Without the framework of the Conflict Cloud, it would not have been possible to develop the Network of Projects solution in such a robust way. Without the creative friction that comes from conflict and without the intrinsic limiting elements we experience in every situation we try and improve, there will never be the signs that lead to a systemic solution.

The Thinking Required for Change

The major problem with replacing a hierarchical mindset lies in the subliminal, unchallenged mental models that make us believe that an organization requires a superimposed control mechanism, be it a boss, a function, or an accounting structure based on cost accounting type considerations. The Thinking Processes from the theory of Constraints help us understand the connections, linkages, and the overall mechanism by which we infer reality. Reality is shaped in our minds by connections that largely remain unchallenged unless we unveil them. By making explicit the cause-and-effect relationships with which we perceive reality, we have an opportunity to challenge all of those assumptions that limit our ability, for instance, to work within a non-silo infrastructure, like a network of projects. More in general, if we want an organization where conventional hierarchy has been challenged to function well, we must enable higher forms of organizations as "thinking systems"; attempts to do this are stifled by both current educational systems and the corporate world.

It is not enough simply to change processes or make organizations flatter. Flat organizations could easily turn into a short-lived gimmick unless we *systemically challenge* the working and, ultimately, existential paradigms that govern the image that we have of what it means to live and work together. This requires a considerable cognitive effort; without the right methods to support that effort there can be little guarantee of continued success. The next section is dedicated to explaining how the Thinking Processes from the Theory of Constraints can help to do precisely that.

The Pattern for Change with the Thinking Processes

In the Decalogue approach, all the conversations for action that take place in the network can be transmitted through the use of the Thinking Processes; they provide heightened focus, accelerate discussion and consensus, and provide easy to communicate, visual and verbal results. They are powerful enhancers of Involvement and Flow. Through continued and ongoing use, they can reduce the variation that inevitably arises when points of view and ways of expressing those points of view are allowed to deteriorate. Reducing variation through the Thinking Processes thus increases Quality even at the level of human interaction. They can be used in a continuous cycle, from creating overall long-term strategy, down to the daily guidelines for carrying out repetitive tasks and new tasks alike. They provide a tangible resource to reinforce the systemic nature of the work, and having such a resource is crucial to support the cognitive challenges involved.

By following the logical sequence in the use of the Thinking Processes, as illustrated further on, organizations can shift away from an organizational model that is inhibiting their full potential toward a model based on a network of synchronized projects using the Critical Chain algorithm. The journey starts with the building of a "Core Conflict."

Building the Core Conflict

Using cause-and-effect logic, the building of a Core Conflict provides us with a cognitive snapshot of the current reality of an organization. This is achieved through verbalizing our intuition into four "categories of speech": the "reality" of the conflict between desired reality and undesired reality, the needs underpinning those positions, a common goal, and assumptions (mental models). This action alone is a huge leap forward in our understanding of our situation.

We start by identifying the *Undesirable Effects* (UDEs) that the organization is experiencing in its way of working. This is a list of factors that are creating discomfort and represents the pain or "symptoms" currently present. We may even describe them as *emergent properties* of the network of interactions within the organization. Once identified, these UDEs are summarized into one, overarching UDE that sums up the current, unsatisfactory reality. We then verbalize what a desirable reality would look like. We call these positions in the conflict cloud D and D'. These become the two conflicting positions D and D' of the "Core Conflict Cloud" (Figure 10.1).

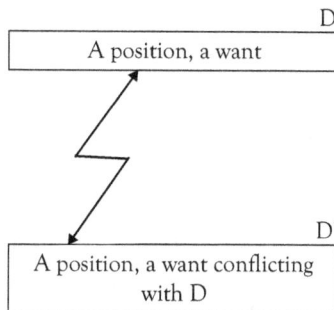

Figure 10.1 Positions D and D' in the Core Conflict

This allows us to move on and identify the profound needs underlying these conflicting positions that drive an organization. We state the need for "control" that forces us to accept or to cope with D; we call it B. Then we state the need for "vision" that prompts us to say that D' is the reality we would like to live in; we call it C (Figure 10.2).

Once these needs are precisely verbalized, the organization can then derive the common goal that satisfies those needs, thus providing an organic direction rather than artificially imposing a goal (A). The needs B and C must be simultaneously satisfied in order to achieve the goal in A (Figure 10.3).

The first phase of building a Core Conflict generally involves a group of leaders and executives who are free to "bitch and moan" until all the UDEs are verbalized and the conflict is built. Verbalizing UDEs is a very "feel good" exercise where everybody agrees that the company is plagued by these effects. These effects are and feel "real" and everybody would like to get rid of them. Summarizing all the UDEs in one single statement is normally a little cumbersome, but it is generally done in a few hours. At this point, the procedure of identifying the desired reality, needs, and goal

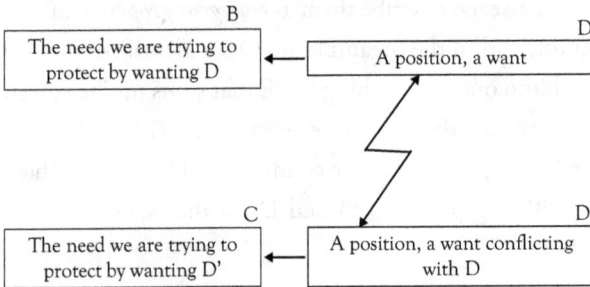

Figure 10.2 The needs B and C

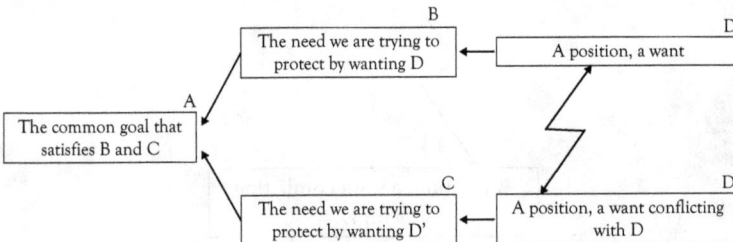

Figure 10.3 The Core Conflict with positions, needs, and goal

begins and the end result is normally welcomed as a breakthrough. How does that breakthrough happen?

The conflict cloud helps to sharpen our intuition. In a very short time, the group of leaders and executives has moved from an often disparate set of nonverbalized hunches to a clear-cut picture of the forces that keep them from achieving their goal. Moreover, a precise description of the needs that craft the psyche of the organization goes a long way toward helping to understand the "why" we are trapped in this conflict, the reason for it. We believe that no top management strategic retreat session delivers a tangible and operational output like this one. Now that the intuition is strong, we can make it stronger.

What transforms a Core Conflict into a full-blown picture of our current reality is a disciplined, orderly elucidation of all the mental models that give birth to the conflict. These mental models are deeply rooted images that we have of ourselves and the world around us. These mental models, which we may also call "assumptions," are the cognitive lenses through which we perceive reality.

Systematically surfacing the assumptions is the most challenging aspect of the Core Conflict because we have to think hard to "smoke them out." Assumptions are, like any other mental construction, the result of factors that are external (the environment, education, experiences, values, etc.) and internal (the chemistry and physics of our mind). The difference between an assumption and a statement of reality is only the realm of validity and this is determined often by cultural circumstances. A practical example of this would be to take a sentence like "In a democracy every citizen is entitled to decent, affordable and reliable healthcare…" and ask for a comment from a statistically representative sample of individuals in the United States, Canada, and Europe.

Assumptions are the logical connectors between goal, needs, and wants; they help us see the logic that shapes the conflict. A conflict with its set of clearly verbalized assumptions portrays the current reality precisely in the way we experience it and is the strongest possible support we can provide to our intuition (Figure 10.4).

Goal, needs, wants, and assumptions tell us why we are in the current state of reality. But they also pave the way to come out of this reality and move toward a future that is more desirable.

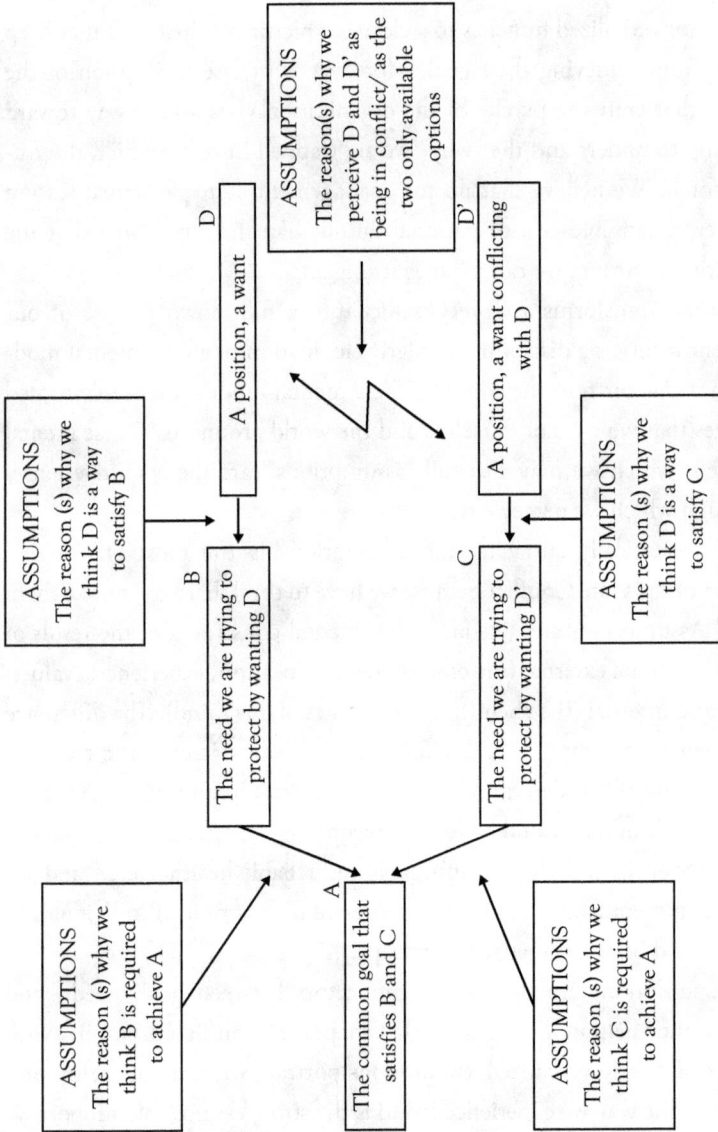

Figure 10.4 Conflict with assumptions

As we said, assumptions are mental models that we have about the world; they are formed as a result of experiences and sociocultural circumstances. Assumptions are, in every respect, a reality for the person that develops them. These assumptions, particularly the ones that we verbalize between D and D' in the conflict, are, *de facto*, the constraining element of our reality; they are our *cognitive constraint*.

Once completed, the Core Conflict provides us with a clear understanding of the prevailing mental models (assumptions) that are keeping the organization stuck on the path toward its goal. This corresponds with the first phase of change: "What to change."

Finding the Breakthrough Solution with "Injections"

By systematically invalidating the assumptions between D and D', it is possible to verbalize "Injections" to the conflict. An injection is a systemic solution that is derived organically by challenging the assumptions between D and D' with logically valid statements that respect the needs expressed in B and C. This is where breakthrough solutions can be developed. The more "core" is the conflict, the more powerful the solutions must be. It is important to be rigorous about injections; in order to qualify as "assumption sweepers," these statements disproving our assumptions must fulfill two prerequisites (Figure 10.5):

1. They must logically invalidate one or more assumptions.
2. They must protect/address both needs OR one of them and be neutral to the other.

Injections are solutions to the conflict; by invalidating all the assumptions, they "evaporate" the conflict cloud (D and D' disappear) and can

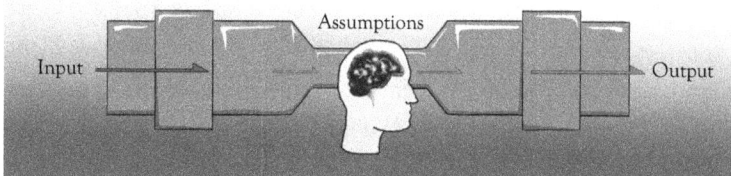

Figure 10.5 Cognitive Constraint

potentially move us from our Current Reality to a more desirable, less constraining Future Reality.

However, in order for this to happen, we have to ensure that this set of Injections is as comprehensive and as free as possible from potential negative implications. Only then will we have a full *understanding* of the pattern in front of us. Only then will we have a thorough comprehension of all the potential ramifications of the solutions we identified (the Injections).

The Future Reality Tree

These solutions/Injections are then connected together using the Future Reality Tree (FRT). The FRT corresponds with the second phase of change, "What to Change to." Using a logic of sufficiency, this process maps out the solutions in a progressive and integrated pattern toward the goal previously identified in the Core Conflict.

The FRT strives to ensure the completeness of the set of Injections identified, hence providing a conceptually reliable path to the future. The process of building an FRT requires some skill, a bit of experience, and a fierce determination. It is in no way an academic exercise nor is it an exercise in conventional logic. Building an FRT is only possible if we have embraced the vision and the method that supports it; the vision is that of a company that takes very seriously its commitment to the future and that sees itself as an ongoing generator of wealth for all its stakeholders and society at large. The method is the orderly, relentless identification of all the cause-and-effect relationships that are likely to shape the future if certain actions are carried out successfully. In this sense, the FRT is similar in nature to the Plan-Do-Study-Act (PDSA) cycle because it prompts a rigorous, scientific investigation of the subject matter.

Once we have built the FRT, we can use the Thinking Processes known as Prerequisite Tree and Transition Tree to ensure that we carry out a series of effective actions that are consistent with the solutions we have identified so that we can transform them into reality. We have described these Thinking Processes in detail in our books *Sechel: Logic, Language and Tools to Manage Any Organization as a Network* (Intelligent Management Inc. 2011) and *Quality, Involvement, Flow: The Systemic Organization* (CRC

Press 2016). Here is a brief summary of how the Thinking Processes work together to create a complete cycle of Transformation.

Summary of the Cycle of the Thinking Processes in the Decalogue

By following the logical sequence in the use of the Thinking Processes, organizations can shift away from an organizational model that is inhibiting their full potential toward a model based on a network of synchronized projects using the Critical Chain algorithm. The cycle of Thinking Processes moves an organization through the three phases of change as identified in the Theory of Constraints: *What to Change, What to Change To, How to Make the Change Happen.*

What to Change:

- Identify the "UDEs" of the organization (symptoms of current reality).
- Summarize into one, overarching UDE that sums up the current, unsatisfactory reality.
- Verbalize what a desirable reality would look like so we now have the two conflicting position of the "Core Conflict."
- Identify the profound needs underlying these conflicting positions (control and vision) and the Goal common to them.
- Surface systematically all the underlying assumptions (mental models) that connect the statements contained in the conflict.

What to Change To:

- Systematically invalidate the assumptions between D and D' to achieve "Injections" (systemic solutions that respect the needs expressed).
- Connect Injections together using the FRT.

How to Make the Change Happen:

- Build a Prerequisite Tree to obtain a map of Intermediate Objectives for every Injection.

- Build a Transition Tree for each Intermediate Objective
  (where needed) to identify tasks.
- Trim potential negative implications stemming from performing tasks (or, more conventionally, from the injections
  developed)
- Schedule—These tasks, free from negative implications, can
  then be scheduled into a project using Critical Chain.
- Repeat—The cycle of Thinking Processes can be repeated
  on an ongoing basis, thus conforming to the PDSA cycle
  of continuous improvement advocated by Dr. Deming
  (Figure 10.6).

Understanding, Knowledge, and Science in a Conscious Organization

Accomplishing the organizational transformation required for all organizations to fulfill their role of sustainable wealth creation does call for
a higher and better use of our intellect. The thinking leveraged by the
Thinking Processes designed by Dr. Goldratt is critical to this end. Understanding and knowledge must be solidly linked to the scientific approach
and the wealth of discoveries it has generated in the last 350 years and that
it continues to generate.

The essence of this scientific approach is embodied in the PDSA cycle,
advocated by Dr. Deming as the main mechanism to generate and sustain
the application of knowledge within any organization. Each of the four
steps of this cycle must be guided by statistical insight. The PDSA cycle
is rooted in the epistemological belief that phenomena must be described
and understood in statistical terms; this statistical vision of the world,
largely applied in the investigation of the natural world, has been adopted
by organizations in a limited way and completely misapplied or ignored
by economists and financiers, not to mention accountants.

An organization with a high level of consciousness has, by definition,
a high level of interconnection with those who work within its system,
with those who supply it, and with those who are its end users. The ongoing task is to constantly satisfy better the needs for control and vision of
those who work within the organization and of those who interact with

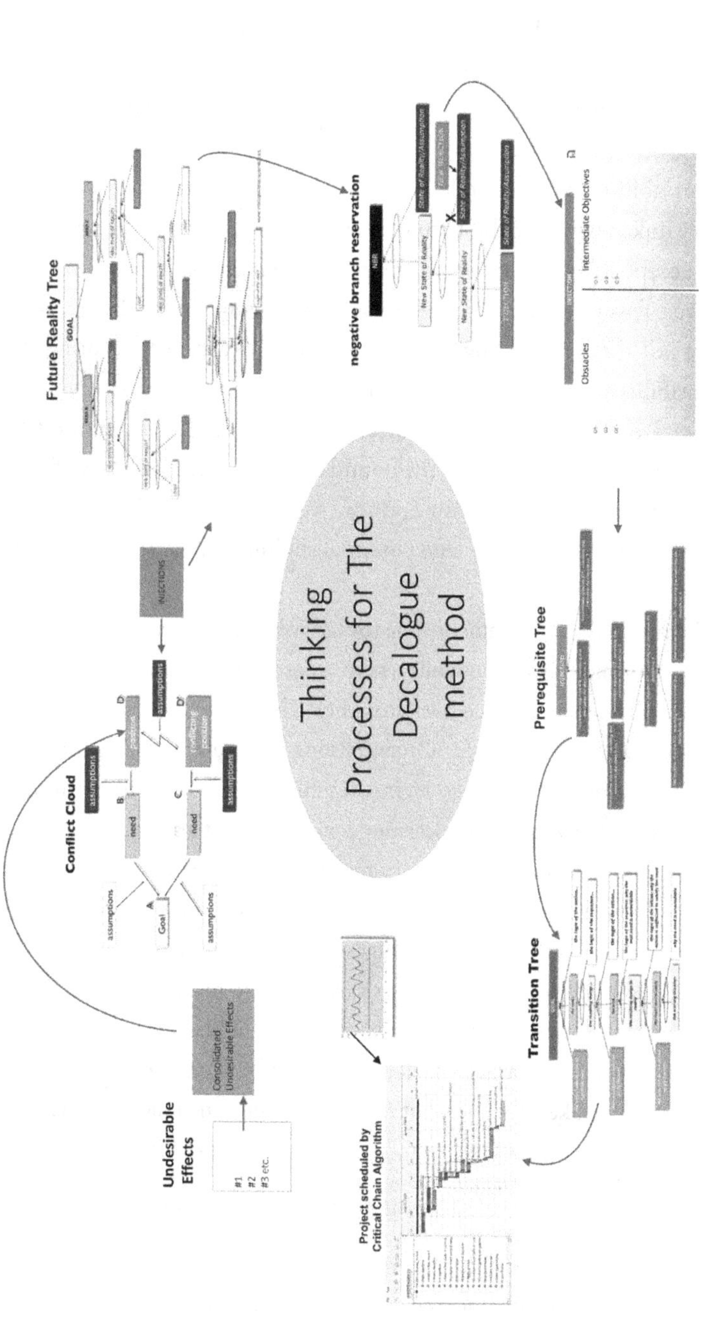

Figure 10.6 The cycle of thinking processes as used in the Decalogue method

it up and downstream, throughout the entire value chain. The inevitable outcome of this level of consciousness and connection is a more *ethical* way of operating. There is automatically no space or use for hedging and price wars, or for pollution of the environment. The inevitable outcome is enterprise with a conscience.

Our ability to create and thrive within this kind of organization is directly linked with our ability to increasingly *do who we are*. This requires us to accept a level of personal freedom to which few are accustomed and even fewer feel comfortable with. This does not mean laissez-faire: it does not mean just doing whatever you want. It means accepting the responsibility of understanding that our only true limits are ourselves and what we are able to perceive for ourselves. Our limits are mental models, and our mental models dictate the boundaries of our actions. As we begin to challenge these models/assumptions, we begin to taste the vivifying experience of exploring our true potential. Fulfilling that potential is not a question of luck but one of choice.

The prevailing management style (or lack of it) has taken the separation between knowledge and consciousness to an extreme and impaired people's ability to choose intelligence over stupidity. This ability needs to be given back and enhanced manifold. Organizations must overcome the damage caused by this disconnection by leveraging this intrinsic unity between consciousness and knowledge, by relearning how to connect learning and choice, and by retooling its people's ability to manage intelligently. A new covenant is required, one where each individual has the opportunity to better themselves and, in so doing, better their organization. We have the intuition, we have the understanding, and we have the methods to make it happen. However, in order for the transformation to truly take hold, we need to create a new kind of leadership and that leadership must be the expression of a new Economics. We take a look at what that can mean in the following chapter.

Closing the Gap

No matter what we try and achieve, there will always be a gap between what we perceive is possible and what we are able to bring into reality. That is the human experience. It is also why we chose the logo we did that includes the shape of the Hebrew letter *hei*.

When we act on the physical world, we change it and transform it, but sooner or later we find an insurmountable barrier, something unbridgeable between our own inner truth and an obstinate external reality. This gap is between thought and action.

Symbolically, the letter *hei* represents the human effort to close the gap, completing the work to help transform the world into what it can potentially become. In other words, bringing heaven down to earth through our actions.

We have to keep trying to improve, but it is our very knowledge of the gap between what we are and what we ought to be that makes us able to be productive partners in the co-creation of this world. It's a lifetime's work. It never ends.

Often, the main obstacle lies in our inability to change the way we perceive and think about things. Most of our work at Intelligent Management is helping people to make that cognitive leap. When we educate ourselves to think and act systemically, we become capable of so much more than we imagine. As Einstein put it, "Those who think it's not possible shouldn't disturb those who are doing it."

Summary of Chapter 10

- Everything that happens in a company is the end result of thinking and, more often than not, this thinking can be vague.
- Systemic thinking skills can be learned.
- The Thinking Processes developed by Dr. Eliyahu Goldratt enhance people's ability to think systemically, both individually and as a group.
- Over-reliance on linear thinking is dangerous in a complex world.
- The systemic methodology for management developed by Intelligent Management approaches complexity from a *non-linear* standpoint.
- The evolution that takes us from silos toward a network requires not just a shift in how we organize our work but in *how we think*.

- Conflict is an opportunity for creativity, and the Conflict Cloud from the Theory of Constraints is a powerful Thinking Process to leverage conflict as an opportunity for breakthrough and innovation.
- The Thinking Processes from the Theory of Constraints provide a complete path for systemic transformation.

CHAPTER 11

Leading the Transformation for the Digital Age

We've got a problem: we are overheating, overproducing, overcrowding. Who is going to fix all that? An Actor? Probably not. You know who can do it? Business, and I know who can help them do it.

—SAP commercial

The upbeat advertisement from SAP is right. Undoubtedly, Business can help with fixing many of the problems the world is experiencing. However, businesses also contribute to many of those problems when they fail to see the systemic implications of their actions. The same can be said of technology. It can be of enormous benefit and we could not imagine our lives today without it. However, for technology to be *meaningful* and not just further complicate people's lives, it needs to be consistent with the goal of an organization and it must alleviate existing restrictions.

A C-Suite with a Clear Purpose

Transformation requires not just technology but new thinking, new methods, and a new outlook. That is the only way we will be able to accomplish what is needed: *transformation of the prevailing silo-based management style into one of whole system optimization.* This transformation is no longer a choice; digital technology is making it unavoidable and it is dictating the pace.

Transformation requires relentless effort, but ultimately, it allows organizations to consistently fulfill their role in the world with the highest quality and speed. This requires knowledge, method, and tools, and it requires a special kind of leader.

Anyone who has any experience with leadership in corporate life cannot fail to see how profoundly damaged this life can be. The kind of interaction that creates a cage for CEOs and Boards is often surreal and sadly too often tragic for all the *stake*holders. Just to make sure we are clear: CEOs spend a lot of their time trying to prove to the Board and the investors they represent that what the company is doing makes sense; in order to do so, they meet with the Board three or four times a year and engage in conversations that span from strategy to GAAP-based financial results. Indeed, Boards are only privy to what the CEO (and the CFO) wants them to know; the financial transparency is guaranteed by some audit subcommittee and the strategy is discussed by people that, more often than not, have mental models that are the reason for which they have been summoned. Doesn't that sound a bit like Enron?

It doesn't have to be like that. The Conflict Cloud we looked at for complexity, hierarchy, and change can be used very specifically in the setting of any organization to capture their specific *Core Conflict*, i.e., the inherent conflict of that particular organization. Once that has been captured and the assumptions are surfaced, we have the possibility to develop a full, systemic set of "injections" to those assumptions. Another way of saying it is: we now see clearly what is keeping us stuck and, logically, we also know how to come out of the "swamp" we are in.

The path out of the swamp, or any path forward, must be sustained by a clearly elucidated cause–effect map. This map must provide

(a) Some epistemological (knowledge-based) rigor
(b) Some ability to predict the outcome of the actions to be taken
(c) A realistic schedule of how and when these actions will be taken

This is what we have labeled as "Projects."

Intrinsically, the work of any organization is made up of *the network of all the projects that emerge from the injections to a well-articulated core conflict*. The role of Leadership (Board and C-suite) in this context is therefore very clear. It is to

(a) Create the environment for these projects to be conducted successfully
(b) Supervise their execution
(c) Intervene in a timely manner with corrective actions triggered by unanticipated statistical fluctuations
(d) Ensure that every stakeholder benefits from the success of the projects

If somebody is willing to spell out the basic (very few) details for a Board to operate in this way, we will be able to spare ourselves much of the chatter on corporate governance that currently clouds the issue.

This transformation is neither easy nor for the fainthearted and it is only possible if we recognize and embrace the new paradigm of interconnectedness we live in. Recognizing the emergence of a new paradigm is very difficult and takes time; but it also takes a new kind of intelligence, one that is capable of understanding the multidimensionality of the implications of our choices: physical, mental, and spiritual.

It is not just about seeing the forest where everyone else only sees trees, it is about understanding the forest as the *emergent property* that is generated when a number of trees grow together.

Leading with Knowledge and Intelligence

For leaders to lead in a systemic way with knowledge, they must have appropriate methods and tools. These methods and tools must be completely in line with the systemic essence of an organization; they cannot be separate (or contradictory). They can have a technical content but they cannot be techniques; they must be a direct emanation of a way of thinking. Moreover, they should enhance and increase people's systemic intelligence through their use.

When presented with some sort of "Quality improvement toolkit," Dr. Deming was almost invariably dismissive as he perceived them as either unnecessary or conceptually wrong. Apart from a tepid endorsement of the Ishikawa diagram for cause–effect analysis, Deming only relied on predictive statistics studies (SPC) and its natural companion, the Process Improvement Chart, at the time simply called Control Chart.

Why is process improvement and managing variation through SPC so important? Leaders and managers need to be able to make rational decisions about their organizations, and the work of their organizations consists of processes. Therefore, managers should know how processes behave, both now and in the future. Whether they are aware of it or not, all processes are affected by variation.

Why should an executive go to the trouble of understanding the statistical behavior of any process? To understand this fully, we have to make a distinction between forecasting and predicting. Executives may be asked to make forecasts, and these are empirical suppositions based on previous evidence and, in many cases, fears and hopes. The usefulness of such forecasts is limited, and reliance on them perpetrates a totally inadequate empirical approach to management. Executives, instead, need to be able to predict how any given process will behave in the future as a result of their decisions. This prediction must be grounded in statistical understanding and the epistemological stance it portrays. Statistical Predictability means that the process oscillates "predictably" within its upper and lower limits of variations. *This is the only kind of prediction that leaders and managers can reasonably make and the only one that gives rational value to their decisions*, as opposed to management based on hunches.

SPC and process improvement charts are indeed the very backbone of any systems-building exercise as they provide insight, not just numbers. (See Step 3 of the Decalogue methodology in Chapter 3.) SPC shelters us from the risk of "linear thinking"; it avoids the mental trap of spreadsheet-fueled, deterministic calculations that are blindsided to speed of flow and systemic implications. Indeed, when properly absorbed and used, SPC is never a technique; it is, as Dr. Deming has said, a way of thinking.

Moreover, seeing systemic implications opens us up to understanding the importance of collaboration beyond the boundaries of our own organizations.

Leading with Critical Chain

Statistical predictability in the processes making up an organizational system facilitates greatly the creation of a network of projects. We can create this network by leveraging the power of the finite capacity scheduling underpinned by the Critical Chain approach to managing projects.

Critical Chain represents the embodiment of a vision of the organization based on pace of flow, people's involvement, and great emphasis on quality. Quality, involvement, and flow are the basic philosophical pillars of the systemic organization, so Critical Chain plays a major role in the building of an intrinsically systemic organization.

Organizations that are functional/hierarchical grids are clearly inadequate because of their inability to fully support, measure, and promote intrinsically cross-functional activities. They trap the potential of their people into silos. The solution is to design organizations as a network of interdependent projects that work together to achieve the goal of the organization. The allocation of people to tasks according to their skills and level of competency unlocks their potential. It produces an effective use of the resources available, a more ethical consideration of people's capabilities, and allows us to unleash the power provided by the "intelligent" implementation of project management. Critical Chain enables all this to happen methodologically and practically.

When we combine Critical Chain with the use of SPC, we equip leaders with a "dashboard" that enables them to have real-time monitoring and control of what is going on inside their organization, allowing them to understand what really matters: the state of the Project Buffers.

Designing organizations as networks of projects is not just important for organizations as individual entities; it equips them structurally, operationally, and cognitively to optimize their interactions with larger networks of value.

Leading with Intelligent Emotions

It is not possible to trigger a better functioning of our intelligence without some sort of handle on our emotions. We have come to call the ability to harness the power of our emotions to propel the rational side of ourselves *Intelligent Emotions*. A leader above all needs to develop these.

This brings us back to the Conflict Cloud. Emotions manifest themselves in the form of the mental models, or assumptions, that link the elements of a Conflict Cloud. The states of reality typified by the conflicting positions in a cloud exist as a result of some level of "amplification" of the needs for security and satisfaction; this amplification creates the "separation," what we experience as "conflict." For instance, when we focus on our fears or decide to exercise restraint, we almost invariably end up justifying "not doing" something, to maintain the situation the way it is. On the other hand, when we pay attention to our satisfaction, when we focus on the fulfillment of our desires, we become prone to wanting "to do" something. Both the neurology and the metaphysics of this phenomenon are a fascinating field of investigation.

The mental models that constitute these amplifiers, as well as the ones that underpin the conflicting positions in a cloud, are the emotions that we want to harness. Why? Because if left to themselves, they would single-handedly jeopardize any attempt at managing the variation and the synchronization that our organization so painstakingly pursues. Unguarded and unchecked emotions can be vital for some artistic (not necessarily creative) endeavors but can easily disrupt organizations because they are powerful catalysts of *entropy*. The Thinking Processes from the Theory of Constraints that we looked at in the previous chapter provide a highly practical way of developing intelligent emotions.

In short: Leadership in a complex, network-like environment requires an enhanced kind of systemic intelligence and the ability to master the emotions that are generated by the change underway. The science of management that goes with this intelligence should adopt methods and tools that are consistent and adequate for the work required.

Leading with a New Economics

> *Best efforts and hard work, not guided by new knowledge, they only dig deeper the pit we are in. The aim of this book is to provide new knowledge.*
>
> —W. Edwards Deming, *The New Economics*

Deming's warning was clear. Unless we arm ourselves with new knowledge then, no matter how hard we work, we will only dig ourselves deeper into trouble. Deming provided us with this new knowledge for creating systems-based organizations and this knowledge, in turn, calls for a new economics. Only systemic knowledge and intelligence can enable the new economics and these need to be fostered and groomed. Before we can make it new, what do we mean by "economics"?

Economics belongs to the realm of the "social sciences." It aims at investigating the production, distribution, and consumption of goods and services. Economics also concerns itself with the study of economies and how the players, the decision makers, act to guide economic choices.

At the most fundamental level, economics should pertain to the understanding of how to deal with the resources at hand and optimize their use for a stated goal. In this sense, economics is also a "political science" because the use of these resources should be guided by political decisions. (Indeed, politics should be guided by a philosophical and ethical vision, but this is another story.)

Economics mimics science by developing models, in this case economic models, that should explain the economic outcome of certain decisions and these models are, or should be, inspired by a vision of the world. In recent decades, The Royal Swedish Academy of Sciences has instituted a Nobel Prize for Economics and several economists have been awarded for the models they have developed.

In summary, an economist, hopefully inspired by a vision of the world, develops models that should guide the economies of countries to an optimal utilization of their resources for a stated goal. Governments, hopefully guided by a vision, embrace economic models based on their adherence to their vision.

Where does the problem with models lie? Any model is and must be based on a set of assumptions. When these assumptions are not verified and validated, the model is bound to fail in providing the results it was designed for. Of course, the political circumstances of any democratic country change very frequently and the ability to translate models into effective policy making is always less optimal than one would wish; moreover, an increasingly interconnected world calls for increasingly complex models with assumptions that are harder and harder to validate. Indeed, governments are pressed to take actions and these actions have to accommodate for political agendas that are not necessarily driven by the vision that inspired the economic model. Moreover, when time (and perceived risk/reward) comes into the picture and we slide into the field of "finance," we witness the full potential of the prevailing economic paradigms as reflected in the models that, tragically, still today purport to create value.

If we continue the analysis of this chain of causes and effects, we can understand why the world is experiencing the current economic predicaments.

Why Current Economic and Financial Models
Are Flawed

We need to broaden our view of what economics should be because it affects us all, and leaders in particular. Mainstream economic and financial models, the ones that currently rule the markets and determine value, have shifted their focus over the years. Whereas previously the attention was placed on what was best for the society they were trying to model, now the emphasis is on what it is mathematically possible to achieve for the benefit of a few. It is thanks to mathematics that we understand the physical world and it is thanks to its rigorousness that we are confident that the scientific method can provide acceptable validity. Sadly, the models of most economists and financiers are far from being the offspring of any scientific method.

Current mainstream economic and financial models are flawed for two sets of reasons:

1. They are often divorced from realistic assumptions about the situation they seek to model AND from the managerial actions that should ensure the predicted outcome. In other words, the modeling happens in the vacuum of second tier "mathematical" speculations with flawed assumptions about what is possible or impossible to achieve managerially.

2. Far too many, and often prevailing, economic and financial models pursue an idea of value that is divorced from any concept of the general wealth and well-being of individuals and society. Such models are based on a systematically disproven "rational" behavior that is driven by the desire for individual profit. These models are rooted in the paradigm that if somebody wins somebody else has to lose. They call it "competition" and a gigantic and ineffective apparatus has been created to "ensure" fair competition.

Providing a Sustainable Outlook on Value and Wealth

In order to reassert economics as a useful field of investigation, we have to reground it in a new paradigm; a new economics can only be originated by a new outlook on value and wealth. As Senator Robert F. Kennedy once said, "The GDP cannot be considered a measure for the standard of our lives."

The starting point is to define what the role of the government should be and which policies an economic model should mirror. Any government should first and foremost protect the freedom of its citizens, for sure: freedom from any risk of slavery. Three major factors impact our freedom, other than the ability to protect ourselves from enemies and practice the religion of our choice: freedom from ignorance, freedom from the tyranny of diseases we cannot afford to cure, freedom to start or adhere to ventures, business, or otherwise.

So, the role of the government in establishing and endorsing an economic model is clear: a solid education and research system, affordable health care for everyone, and a network of support for the development of any form of free enterprise.

How we build these systems, how we manage them, and what set of values should inspire them are the kernel of the new economics. Economics, then, really becomes the science that studies how countries should develop.

The new economics should not just be concerned with better mathematical models to portray scenarios; any serious mathematician would always alert decision makers to the probable fallacy of such models. The new economics must be intimately connected with the ways wealth can be created and the best ways to increase the distribution of this wealth.

The world we live in is becoming exponentially more interconnected and wealth (and its creation) is a multifaceted entity. Which is the wealthier country, one where the GDP is high but millions of people cannot afford serious education and health care, or one where the GDP is lower but these "freedom rights" are guaranteed? This conflict exists only because "economics" is anchored to flawed assumptions about wealth and value.

The distribution of wealth, seen as conflicting with the right of the individual to amass personal wealth to the detriment of others, has always been labeled as "socialist" and as such, unsuitable for the free world. The ugly truth is that prevailing economic and financial thinking has led to the squandering of the resources that the planet has available and to the stifling of innovation. This thinking has systematically favored short-term decisions over long-term planning. This thinking has swayed tens of thousands of talented people away from applying their minds to constructive and foundational work and toward the sterile and artificial domain of "financial products." This thinking has led us to believe that we can create something out of nothing.

Never in human history has the word "scarcity" meant so much. Our resources are scarce and we need to learn how to use them; the name of the game of any serious economic effort then becomes "sustainability." The new economics must become the science that studies the optimization of scarce resources and, in order to do so, must tap into the bodies of knowledge that deal with how finite resources can be successfully managed.

The new economics must also be based on the founding assumption that no win can be based on somebody losing; that we are all interdependent and the well-being of individuals is critical for the well-being of society; that wealth must be created in order for it to be distributed and any form of imbalance will soon turn into a global loss; that individual success to the detriment of others cannot be sustained. The new economics is founded on the assumption that individuals, organizations, large systems and networks, and, ultimately, countries are vehicles for the creation and distribution of ideas, products, services that help everyone to live better, more intelligently, and harmoniously with our environment.

The new economics will strive to provide not just mathematical platforms but also the practical means to achieve a meaningful life.

A New Kind of Learning for Complexity and the Problem with Business Schools

Still today, in spite of the acceleration that new technologies are bringing, business schools tend to offer a body of disconnected knowledge taught in a fragmented manner and within the framework of a functional understanding of the life of organizations. With few exceptions, if Deming's work is taught at all, it is labeled as "quality" and this limits the ability to understand his work as a systemic philosophy for business and economics. Similarly, while it is true that Goldratt's book *The Goal* is recommended reading in many schools, it is relegated to "operations" and students are unlikely to deduce from reading this book in isolation just how universally applicable the Theory of Constraints is. (In one surreal conversation, I was asked by the dean of a business school in Canada what Deming and Goldratt had to do with business.)

Even where there are some attempts in schools to include "systems thinking" as a course or module, these lessons are provided alongside traditional financial and management accounting courses and the lingering ghost of "the invisible hand" believed to be regulating the markets. In other words, systems thinking, if offered at all, ironically becomes just another silo. This is also happening in corporations that have introduced systems thinking departments, no doubt with the best intentions but demonstrating a complete lack of understanding of how to apply systemic knowledge operationally. As long as managers are measured on local, siloed efforts, they will be unable to see the real advantage of any systemic approach.

The result, as amply predicted by Dr. Goldratt in his novel *Critical Chain* set in a university, is that MBA students not only end up unable to "connect the dots," they lack the understanding of which dots need to be connected in the first place. Consequently, MBA programs and the like continue to qualify individuals without the knowledge and tools to build, lead, manage, and grow organizations.

The challenge for academic institutions faced with the task of imparting business education is, just as for any organization, a paradigmatic one. And it is based on the same assumptions of organizational design and control. The design factor, in the case of business schools, concerns "the design of the learning pattern" (not just the elements of the learning pattern) and the control aspect is related to the assurance that their students are hired after graduation. Moreover, business school faculties are often populated by academics who may have little direct knowledge of business as they are on an academic career path and that is a very different pattern.

Last, but not least, management is seen by business schools as something connected with economics and finance, with a smattering of operations and some marketing notions. In other words, there is little understanding of the roles that science and neuroscience play in the education of future managers and leaders. The result is the ballooning of fees for courses whose major value lies in the alumni network to which they provide their students access.

We have attempted to capture the conflict that concerns the teaching curriculum of business schools in the conflict cloud (Figure 11.1).

Business School Conflict

Assumption A-B
A curriculum is made up of elements of knowledge (subject matters)

A
Goal

Educate students to become leaders and managers

Assumption A-C
A full education integrates various elements of knowledge

B
Need

Understand the individual elements of knowledge (subject matters) necessary

C
Need

Understand the interconnections among the various elements of knowledge necessary

Assumption B-D
The simplest way to understand/manage the individual elements of knowledge is to break them up into separate courses

Assumption C-D'
The links that create interdependencies exhibit a dynamic that needs to be studied

D
Position

Continue to teach courses based on individual subject matters

D'
Conflicting position

Teach an integrated courseware

Assumptions D-D'
- Dynamically interacting elements of knowledge do not create emergence;
- The assembly of these elements in the current curriculum provides a coherent synthesis;
- Case studies provide insights that students can apply to their reality;
- The theory necessary for business can be found mainly in economics and finance.

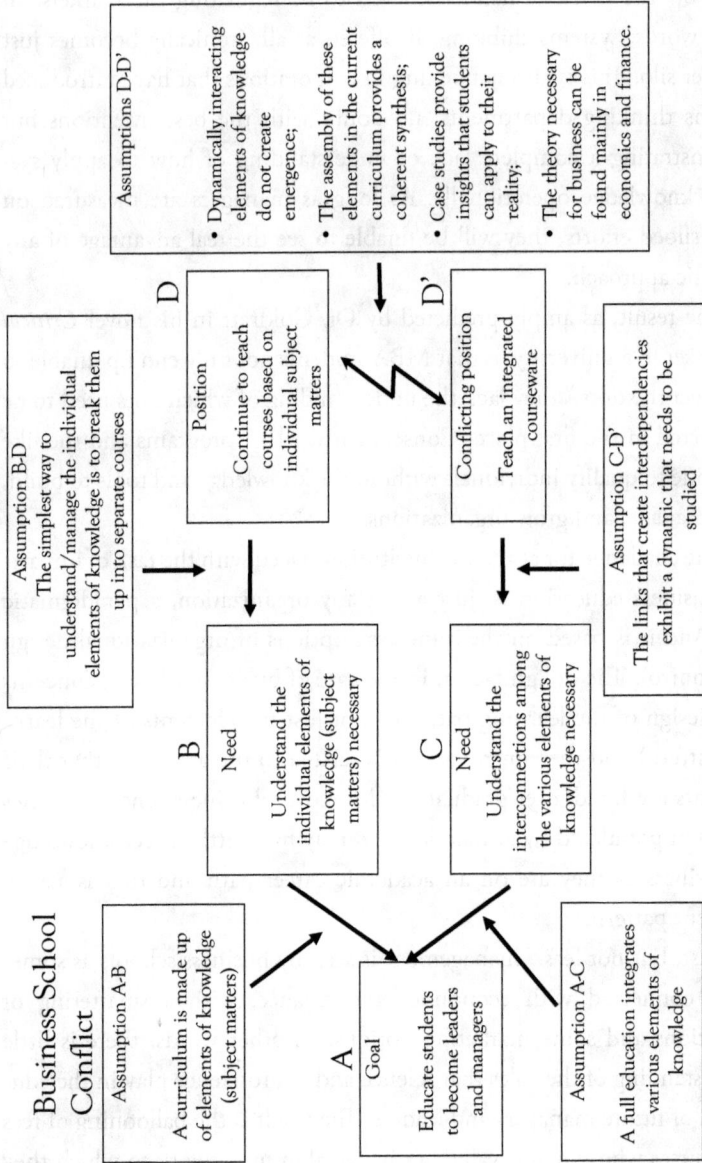

Figure 11.1 The business school conflict

Proposing a New Curriculum for Complexity

If leaders and managers today must be able to understand how things interdepend and evolve in order to navigate complexity, what kind of curriculum should business schools be offering? Whereas students will always need to understand things like marketing and how to read a balance sheet, business schools are not able to offer the subjects in a sufficiently integrated way for today's reality because they are structured hierarchically and in silos. Even if schools consider themselves to be interdisciplinary, this structural limitation prevents them from innovating what they teach and the way they teach it in a significant way. Their courses are offered in "pieces" that are then assembled together, but they never form a holistic whole. I would like to suggest the areas that an adequate program should include.

A New Kind of Thinking

Linear thinking, the kind that is reinforced by vertical hierarchies and that does not look beyond Excel spreadsheets, is inadequate for complexity. Managers today need to be able to think in a radically different way if they are to keep up with and anticipate change. A simplistic way of putting it is to say that they need to be able to connect the dots. An accurate way of describing this is to say they need to be able to think systemically. They need to have a holistic understanding of the reality they are in; they need to know that when they make a decision and act on that decision, there will be repercussions. They need a way to "see" those effects before they happen.

A New Way of Counting

The kind of management accounting that students are taught in MBAs is necessary because of the way tax reporting is done and balance sheets are written. However, it is not the most useful way of understanding cash coming in and cash going out. When managers lose a sense of the real money they are handling (money in and money out) as opposed to accounting numbers, they can put an enterprise at risk.

A New Way of Understanding

A company is made up of processes, such as sales and production. These processes display a behavior and this behavior can be measured. There are statistical methods for understanding precisely whether a process is in statistical control or not. If a manager does not have this detailed level of understanding of the processes under their responsibility, then they cannot possibly know when and if it is the case to make changes for improvement. Without this knowledge, they risk doing more harm than good.

A New Way of Caring

Processes, apart from purely mechanical ones, are operated by humans. As humans, we have fears, desires, needs, and a whole range of emotions. Managers need to be able to interact with their staff on an emotional level, with intelligent emotions, especially in an increasingly digitized and decentralized world. This kind of skill can be learned and developed.

In order for leaders and managers to act proficiently and effectively in today's complex environments, they need to be able to understand and navigate complexity. A curriculum today should therefore

- Enable a systemic understanding of organizations and the interdependencies they are part of
- Teach systemic thinking skills for complexity
- Teach accounting methods for throughput management
- Teach statistical methods to gain real insight into process behavior
- Teach management skills to manage conflicts and interact with staff in a meaningful way

This curriculum for an "MBA for complexity" can be built right away with the Thinking Processes from the Theory of Constraints, Throughput Accounting, and statistical methods that have been around for decades (Figure 11.2).

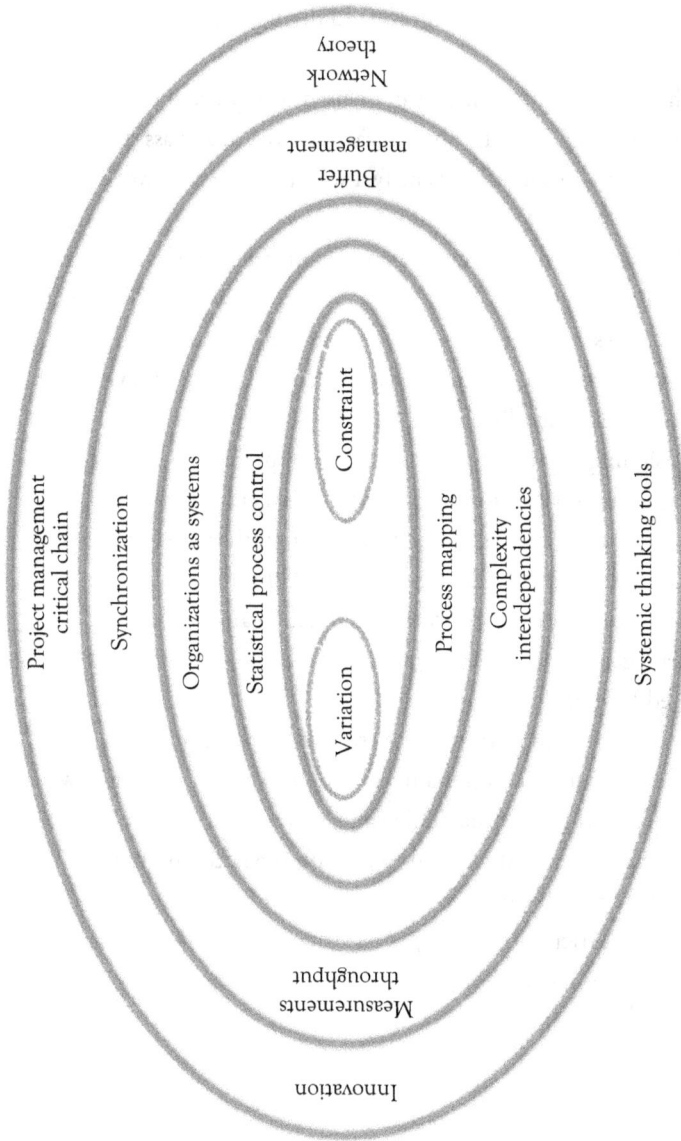

Figure 11.2 A new systemic curriculum for Business Schools

Summary of Chapter 11

- Meaningful technology must be consistent with the goal of an organization and alleviate existing restrictions.
- Transformation is not a choice and digital is dictating the pace.
- The Core Conflict Cloud can be used to capture the inherent conflict of an organization, surface nonverbalized assumptions, and systemically identify a way ahead in a network of projects.
- The Network of Projects organization renders the role of the C-suite radically clear.
- The necessary transformation toward whole system optimization requires a new kind of leadership based on knowledge and systemic intelligence.
- Designing organizations as networks of projects is not just important for organizations as individual entities; it equips them structurally, operationally, and cognitively to optimize their interactions with larger networks of value.
- Statistical Process Control and Critical Chain Project Management form the backbone of the knowledge leaders need for transformation.
- Leaders need to learn to cultivate intelligent emotions.
- Transformation requires a new economics and leads to a new understanding of sustainable value and wealth.
- Business schools are not up to date on the necessary knowledge for transformation.
- A new curriculum is required based on systemic knowledge, understanding, and practices.

CHAPTER 12

Recapping It All: Embracing Complexity in the Digital Age with an Operational Solution

The greatest challenge for organizations today is complexity. This is a word that is often misunderstood. Complexity for organizations means *unprecedented levels of interdependencies*. Companies today face unparalleled degrees of interconnectedness, a fast-growing socioeconomic environment shaped by networks, and the rapidly increasing role that digital and decentralized technology plays in our lives. All these factors call for a major overhaul of how we understand, manage, and operate not just transactions, but entire organizations and value chains. It is an unprecedented challenge.

How can we adapt and compete in an increasingly digital and decentralized world? We have to rethink structurally and operationally the way organizations are designed. A major obstacle is that there is little real understanding in the corporate world of what complexity is, how it originates, and what deep shifts, not just in technologies, techniques, and tactics, are required to operate and innovate in a complex world. Indeed, big names in the consulting world talk about "cutting through" complexity, or breaking it down, revealing a complete lack of understanding of the issues or the concept of *emergence*. Emergence means that there are properties that emerge when parts of a system interact that are not present at the level of the single parts. Every level of complexity gives rise to new emergent properties. This is the sense behind the expression that the whole is greater than the sum of its parts. When we acknowledge this new interpretation of reality, we inevitably see the need for an appropriate way of thinking, organizing, and acting. This cannot be the same way of leading and managing that was appropriate for a mechanistic world.

Unfortunately, organizations (and business schools) are still very much trapped in an outdated paradigm of silos, fragmentation, conflicts, and a zero-sum game. There has not yet been a real shift away from an outdated, deterministic worldview of organizations toward an urgently needed understanding of organizations as one whole system. No matter which techniques forward-looking managers may try to adopt, management remains widely rooted in the idea of command and control, and this is reflected in a traditional, hierarchical/functional organizational design (silo mentality). In reality, the inherent nature of organizations is based on *interactions*. These interactions can be limited to one physical location or distributed over a global network.

The work with my team at Intelligent Management with organizations over the last 20 years has been to challenge the prevailing Newtonian, mechanistic mindset of management and to develop an operational solution that acknowledges the intrinsic nature of organizations as whole systems. The role of leadership for complexity then becomes very clear: to *guide how the network of interdependencies occurs* so that an organization can achieve its maximum potential, beyond any artificial constrictions.

Fundamental Questions for Radical New Answers

Physicists are accustomed to asking themselves very fundamental questions in order to understand nature. When it comes to managing organizations, we have to ask fundamental questions to develop the kind of radical solutions required for our fast-evolving reality. We also need a robust means of investigation to support this work. The Theory of Constraints provides a structured framework for developing and communicating breakthrough solutions with its Thinking Processes. By framing a situation of blockage as a conflict and surfacing the assumptions (mental models) that make the conflict exist, we can systematically challenge outmoded thinking to create real innovation. By real innovation, we mean something that removes an existing limitation.

Let's take the issue of managing complexity and how people try to tackle it. On the one hand, people believe they can manage complexity by breaking it up into its parts, or structures. They adopt this position to protect a legitimate need that we can verbalize as *understand the components*. The opposite, conflicting position is to manage complexity by focusing on the interactions and dynamics, or patterns. The legitimate need that this position tries to protect is to *understand the interdependencies*. We can move forward out of this impasse by challenging the assumptions that keep the conflict in existence. We can summarize these assumptions as (1) the whole is equal to the sum of its parts; (2) no new properties emerge from interactions among the parts; and (3) interactions among the parts are always and only deterministic and linear (mechanistic view). Now that we have verbalized those assumptions and they are "out in the open," we have cleared a path to find a solution that will allow us to lead and manage organizations in a way that is appropriate, adequate, and effective for today's complex reality. But first, we have to look at why organizations are still stuck in the hierarchical/functional model.

Mechanistic Thinking and Silos

The "complexity conflict" is in fact intrinsically connected with why people persist with the hierarchical/functional model. This anachronistic model is related to "understanding the components." It mechanistically divides an organization up into divisions and ranks.

The concept of hierarchy is deeply embedded in our psyches. As far back as biblical times, Moses was advised by his father-in-law, Jethro, to create a hierarchy to help him deliver his teachings to the population more effectively. There was a clear advantage in delegating responsibility in a hierarchical way and it became a standard way to build an organization.

When organizations are created and organized in a matrix of vertical hierarchy and functions, it creates inevitable negative consequences. It causes a series of "walls" or divisions that inhibit the resources involved in producing an optimal result toward the overall goal, communication gets slowed down or completely blocked, innovation struggles to emerge through the ranks and bureaucratic obstacles, projects are delayed and go over budget, quality suffers, and reaction time to changing market demands is too slow.

When it comes to negative effects for people, individuals suffer because they do not have the authority to carry out the tasks for which they are responsible. Careers are limited because people work for a boss who has to improve their own performance in a vertical way. This means that competencies, both technical and managerial, do not find a natural way to develop. This creates frustration due to artificial "ceilings."

Even more dramatically, "silo sickness" means that the larger implications of cause-and-effect relationships that exist in organizations are totally disguised. *It takes time for the effects of a cause to propagate through a system.* People have no means of understanding the implications of their local, siloed decisions for the big picture. Even the heads of functions are blind-sided to them.

Overcoming the Hierarchical/Functional Model with 10 Transformational Steps

Just as with the complexity conflict, there is a conflict that keeps people stuck in adopting a hierarchical/functional model *vs.* not adopting it, and there is a set of assumptions that keeps this conflict in existence.

To move forward, we must question the assumptions, *i.e.*, mental models that create the conflict and keep it alive. Over the years of our on-the-field research and development, at Intelligent Management, we have come to summarize the assumptions that keep the hierarchy conflict alive as

- A hierarchy can only be vertical.
- Control has to be exercised equally over all components of the organization.
- The global optimum is equal to the sum of the local optima.

To challenge these assumptions operationally, we need a plan of action that can transform an organization into a whole system. Our work at Intelligent Management began with the systemic vision of Dr. W. Edwards Deming and statistically controlled processes (Theory of Profound Knowledge) and grew to embrace the concept of managing a constraint (Theory of Constraints). By working on a synergy of these approaches, we discovered a powerful way to orchestrate and synchronize the efforts of an organization toward its goal. We came to see that we could bring together the idea of constraint with the idea of a statistically controlled system. To do that cohesively, we have to orchestrate statistically controlled processes and subordinate them to a well-defined (and very statistically stable) part of our system, the constraint. If these stable, *i.e.*, reliable, well-orchestrated, processes all have the capacity to subordinate to the chosen constraint, then all we need in order to protect the whole system is a "buffer" in front of the constraint; needless to say, the oscillation of the buffer must be controlled statistically. We developed a visualization for the concept of a systemic organization designed around a constraint and we refer to it as the "Systemic Organization Cartoon." The "Cartoon" is illustrated in Figure 12.1 and is inspired by a sketch made by Dr. Deming of "Production Viewed as a System."

We were able to define how to shift an organization operationally away from silos to become a whole system in 10 macro steps that we called "The Decalogue." From a philosophical as well as scientific viewpoint, the Decalogue attempts to shift management from the obsolete, Newtonian worldview in which the results of the whole organization equal the sum of its individual, separate, and hierarchically conceived parts, toward a systemic network made of interdependent components. The shift is achieved by combining the allegedly "reductionist" approach of the Theory of Constraints with a purely systemic view based on interdependencies and interactions. It does so in practical terms by

(a) Building interdependent processes managed through the control of variation

(b) Subordinating these interdependencies to a strategically chosen element of the system called constraint

(c) Designing the organization as a network of interdependent processes and projects managed at finite capacity with a clearly defined common goal

The 10 macro steps of the Decalogue methodology were published in 1999 in *"Deming and Goldratt: The Decalogue."* It was the first book to be published by Dr. Goldratt's publisher about the Theory of Constraints that was not written by Goldratt himself.

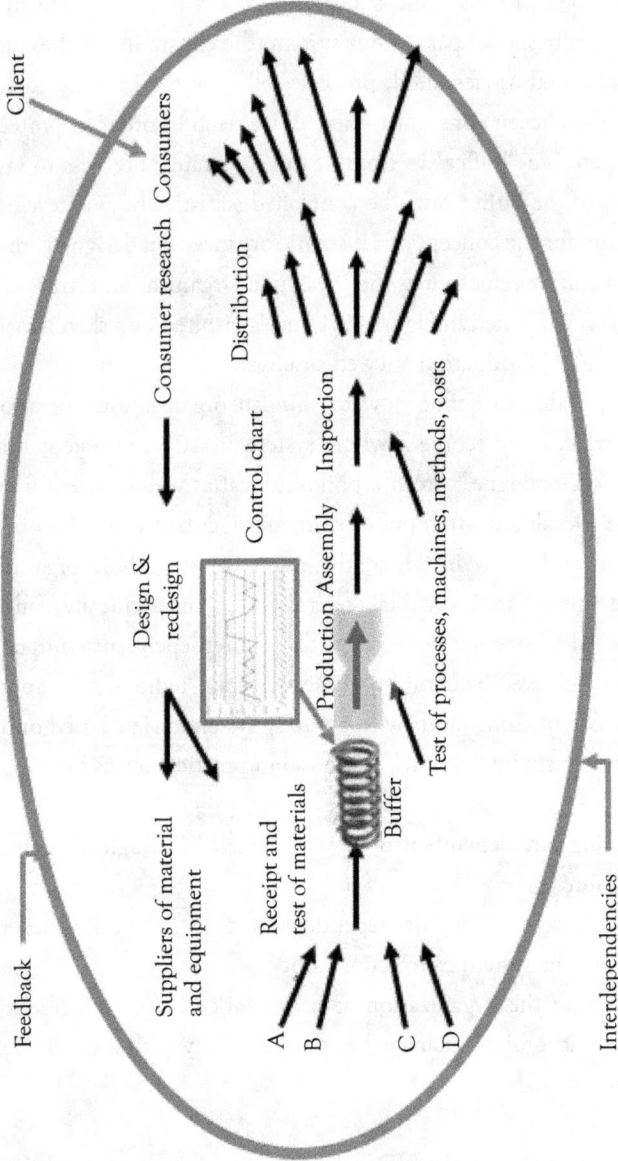

Figure 12.1 The "Systemic Organization Cartoon"

The steps to shift from silos to system are the following:

1. Establish the goal of the system, the units of measurement, and the operational measurement (without a common goal, there is no system).
2. Understand the system (draw the interdependencies).
3. Make the system stable (understand variation and its impact on the network, make sure that the oscillation of the processes is statistically predictable).
4. Build the system around the constraint (subordinate the organization to the constraint, the only part of the system that can never stay idle).
5. Manage the constraint (protect the constraint from the intrinsic variation present inside the system with a "buffer"—buffer management).
6. Reduce variation at (of) the constraint and the main processes (wider variation implies poorer management; low variation improves predictability, reduces inventory and WIP).
7. *Create a suitable management/organizational structure (design the network of interdependencies as a network of projects to improve the performance of the system).*
8. Eliminate the "external constraint" (sell all the capacity the system has available).
9. Where possible, bring the constraint inside the organization and fix it there (an "internal" constraint is much easier to manage than an external constraint).
10. Create a continuous learning program (improve the system through personal improvement).

The Fundamental Constituents of Work

We did not have a complete answer for Step 7 of the Decalogue, "Create a suitable management/organizational structure," when *Deming and Goldratt* was published. Over the years of working with the Decalogue, and, true to our vocation as organizational scientists, with our increasing familiarity with complexity science and Network theory, what emerged was a new organizational design for complexity.

Moving beyond the blockage created by a hierarchical/functional structure is, above all, a *cognitive challenge*. The notion of hierarchy, as we have said, is deeply etched in the human psyche. What we need, then, for a viable solution is something that *preserves the concept of hierarchy but that shapes it in a completely different way.*

In order to generate a solution for a *suitable organizational structure*, we needed to ask fundamental questions about what work actually is as opposed to how it is carried out in most organizations today. This is the only way we can avoid making the same assumptions we have made in the past and repeating the same errors. By answering accurately the question "What is an organization?" we can understand both conceptually and on a practical, day-to-day level the most effective way to manage.

When we overcome a limited and utterly deterministic perspective, when we put aside the artificial distinctions and barriers that result from silo thinking, we can take a much deeper look. We can then identify the basic elements that make up the life of an organization. At the most basic, elementary particle-like level, what do leaders and managers have to deal with? We can boil it all down to four things:

1. The elements of the system under the responsibility of leadership
2. How these elements interact to produce the desired outcomes
3. The context within which elements and their interactions play out, in other words, the market
4. All the stakeholders—board, investors, employees, society at large

These four constituents form the essential core of leading and managing an organization. In order to cope with the ever-growing complexity of these four constituents, an astonishing number of techniques have been developed to help leaders navigate the agitated waters of the corporate world. Many of these techniques have merit and some of them are certainly more than a palliative. A technique, however, is only a partial remedy. What is lacking is an approach that (a) helps to understand better each of these four constituents and (b) provides a *unified vision* and a corresponding method to tackle them.

New Awareness About Interactions

The elements of a network, their interactions, the common goal they pursue, and the context within which they exist do not have to be dealt with in isolation. We began to see that there is a way out of the blind alley of organizational divisiveness that stems from artificial silos and it begins with understanding that company functions should be seen in a very different way. They should be perceived as *a repository of competencies or subject matter expertise.* In other words, they contain the know-how needed in order to achieve the tasks at hand.

These tasks, no matter how difficult or complex, require some form of interdependence with other sets of competencies; accordingly, organizational design only makes sense when it concentrates on creating the best, easiest, and smoothest way to allow these competencies to interact.

Interact for what? To achieve a common goal; invariably, this goal is connected with satisfying the Market. Only when we truly understand what an organization is can we design one. Organizations are *whole systems.* Organizational design, then, is the science, not the magic, of enabling different competencies to achieve the goals for which they have been brought together.

A New Organizational Design: The Network of Projects

How can we best allow competencies to interact? Essentially, any organization is engaged in two kinds of activities: *repetitive processes* and *one-off projects.* Repetitive processes, such as closing the books or performing scheduled maintenance, lay the foundation for the life of the organization. This is what statistical understanding is all about: ensuring the reliability, dependability, and predictability of processes. This is the very fabric of quality.

One-off projects are what propel the organization to success; new ideas, new technologies, innovation, experimentation are the *raison d'être* for any organization. However, they are only possible and produce results when they emerge from strong roots in quality.

Process and projects have very many things in common; they both are, essentially, a set of activities aimed at a very well identified goal. Both have, in general, a timeline for their execution and both need to be operated with a certain degree of statistical predictability in order to be effective (and cost effective).

Unlike repetitive processes that are often confined to functions, Projects take the predicaments of a siloed structure to a new and different level, and for the following two reasons:

1. A project is, by definition, a one-off activity and, more often than not, draws resources from a variety of company functions, in this way *increasing the need for collaboration among people accustomed to working and thinking locally.*
2. A project is often something that brings innovation, a positive disruption in the life of the organization. Cognitively, a project challenges, albeit in a desirable way, the all too human tendency to resist change in an organization.

A project, in other words, exposes in a blatant and somewhat "violent" way how impossible it is for a conventionally hierarchical structure to accommodate the flow of activities.

Logically, *if* the essence of an organization is the projects (and processes) it is made up of *and* project buffers offer a very effective real-time way to monitor the overall impact of actions taken toward the goals that the organization is pursuing, *then* it makes a lot of sense to consider an organizational design that reflects the very nature of the work the organization does. We call this design *the Network of Projects.*

What we advocate is the transformation of the conventional silo-based hierarchy into an organization where there is full systemic optimization, made up of projects and processes, where the control mechanism is the management of buffers through statistical understanding. In this organizational design, company functions are seen exclusively as *pools of competencies.* These competencies are allocated to projects using a mechanism based on finite capacity, that is, we never schedule a resource simultaneously on two different tasks, we forfeit multitasking in favor of stacking activities, and we foster a culture of promptness as opposed to procrastination (student syndrome). This can be achieved effectively through the Critical Chain Project Management method from the Theory of Constraints. Critical Chain becomes, then, much more than simply an algorithm to accelerate project completion; it is the vehicle to integrate, control, and deploy the resources/competencies of the organization.

What does the Network of Projects organization look like? Instead of company functions, there are networks of projects; instead of heads of functions, there are managers of increasingly complex projects that draw their resources from a pool of available competencies with no resource contention; instead of executives that fight for power, there is cooperative work that is in sync with the goal of the company. Instead of often-conflicting local indicators of performance, there is one single driver for everybody.

In this systemic organization as a Network of Projects, leaders will be the enablers of meaningful and market-driven projects and will foster a new organizational climate, one of cooperation and win–win.

The Network of Projects that makes up the life of the organization is a particular kind of network, called directed network, where the "direction" is provided by the goal of the organization. Such networks are called scale free, with a hierarchy of hubs and nodes. Accordingly, in an organization there will be *hub-projects*, namely the ones more relevant for the success of the organization, and *node-projects*, *i.e.*, projects that are smaller but still necessary for the development of the organizational network. What ensures the connection among these hub and node projects is the finite capacity algorithm for their synchronization (Critical Chain) fueled by an appropriate database of resources. (Figure 12.2 depicts the Network of Projects synchronized through Critical Chain.)

Stated simply, two key elements enable the optimal management of finite resources: *predictability* in the execution of activities and their *synchronization*. In other words: IF individual activities are performed with a high degree of reliability, with quality, AND these activities are orchestrated with a powerful algorithm that allows the best possible synchronization toward the stated goal, THEN we have an infrastructure that can maximize the throughput that the organizational system can generate.

In a systemic organization, anyone, at any time, is part of a project. They lend their competence to a project that is designed, along with all the other projects the company is made up of, to maximize the results of the whole company toward its goal. Every member of staff at any given time is a resource for a project or a Project Manager for a project; sometimes they are one or the other on multiple projects. Some people will develop competencies for managing increasingly complex projects, some others

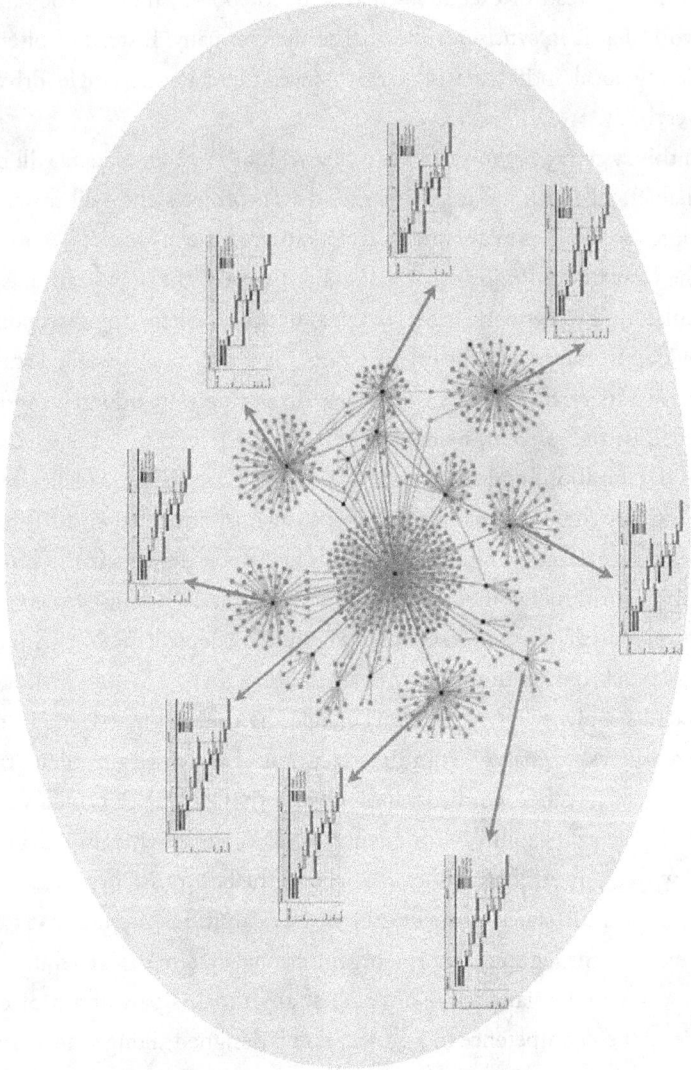

Figure 12.2 Depiction of the Network of Projects

will continue to deepen their competencies and enrich the content base of the company. Most importantly, all of them will naturally be placed within a continuous learning pattern to strengthen the cognitive skills necessary for continuous innovation.

The Mindset Necessary for Digital and Decentralized Enterprises

Digitization is accelerating a shift toward decentralization. What businesses increasingly need to consider is how their production supply chain is integrated with a digital supply chain, and beyond that, their interdependencies within entire supply chains or supply networks.

Once we have freed ourselves from the notion of mechanistic, siloed enterprises and we adopt the idea of *the enterprise as a system, operated as a Network of Projects*, we unleash potential in a way that has not yet been possible. We give individuals the opportunity to develop their competencies beyond the confines of functions. We create space for emergent properties to exist. We can go beyond the boundaries of single companies and create products and services through *networks of companies*, drawing on a much broader pool of competencies scheduled into finite capacity projects. We overcome the boundaries of geography and fiefdom to achieve a global goal.

To achieve this reality requires a higher form of intelligence and ethical awareness and ability to go beyond a localized "what's in it for us" mentality. We can accomplish this with the ecology of the mind that systemic thinking provides, and by embracing the values of a worldview where profit and the common good are inextricably interdependent. Both W. Edwards Deming and Eliyahu Goldratt understood that humanity is capable of so much more than we imagine. Whatever situation or business we are in, we can do significantly better, and we can achieve that in a meaningful way, not to the detriment of others, but by creating something new, superior, and from which all will benefit, from the supplier to the end user and throughout the supply network. This requires new economic and political thinking beyond national boundaries. Far from being a utopia, this understanding is rapidly becoming the obvious solution, because it is the only sustainable way ahead.

Summary of Chapter 12

- To adapt and compete in an increasingly digital and decentralized world, we have to understand complexity and rethink structurally and operationally the way organizations are designed.
- Organizations are *whole systems*. Only when we truly understand what an organization is can we design one.
- An organization is
  o A network
  o Part of a larger network of value
- Mechanistic thinking and silos are what keep organizations trapped in a traditional hierarchical/functional model where silos exist.
- It is possible to overcome silos and the artificial limitations of the hierarchical/functional model with a whole system perspective and method.
- Leaders and managers have to deal with four fundamental constituents of work that are increasingly complex. These four constituents are
  1. The elements of the system under the responsibility of leadership
  2. How these elements interact to produce the desired outcomes
  3. The context within which elements and their interactions play out, in other words, the market
  4. All the stakeholders—board, investors, employees, society at large
- With a systemic perspective, the focus shifts toward awareness about interactions.
- A new organizational design for complexity that overcomes silos can be found in the Network of Projects.
- Leading and working in increasingly digital and decentralized enterprises is a cognitive challenge and requires a new, systemic mindset.

Appendix

Measurements from the Theory of Constraints

The Theory of Constraints allows us to further simplify our management efforts by providing the fundamental set of measurements (Throughput Accounting) that allows us to understand how our system as a whole is performing:

Throughput (T) is the rate at which the system produces units of the goal (through sales, in For-Profit organizations). Throughput equals the sales revenues (S) minus the totally variable cost (TVC) of what it pays (often out to suppliers) to produce the goods or services sold ($T = S - $TVC).

Inventory (I) is the money tied up in the system to be transformed later into sales. This money is, in most part, in the form of what is generally understood as raw material. Inventory is valued at the cash outlay associated with its procurement. It does not include any allocation from overhead or fixed expense.

Operating Expense (OE) is the money the system spends/invests in generating units of the goal, such as rent, utilities, taxes, payroll, maintenance, advertising, training as well as investments in buildings, machines, etc.

Throughput accounting, unlike traditional accounting, recognizes that time is an important element in Throughput generation. Its measurements provide a meaningful report of cash in and cash out (no accounts receivable/payable are considered until they "materialize" as cash intake/outlay), and it supports a worldview based on consistently increasing performance as opposed to cost reduction. As such, it is completely interconnected with all other activities within an organization and provides an important support for decision making in every aspect of how the system operates.

Statistical Process Control: Control Charts and Reducing Variation

Control charts are a tool devised to measure and improve the variation of processes. They were developed by Walter Shewhart in the 1920s as a result of his work at Bell Laboratories. The control chart offers a much fuller picture than commonly used comparison of data to specifications or to average values of performance. These measurements will only tell us if performance is in or out of specs, above or below average. They tell us nothing about the process which produces these values.

At first glance, a control chart resembles a time series graph. In such a graph, monthly sales, for example, we plot months of the year along the horizontal axis and the number of products sold along the vertical axis. However, as a time series graph only allows comparisons between single values, it does not give us sufficient information about the behavior of a process.

The control chart, which in every respect is a *process behavior chart*, instead puts this information into a context by adding three horizontal lines. The central line acts as a reference against which we identify trends. The other two lines are control limits—the upper and lower control limits, or *natural process limits*. (These are calculated with the help of coefficients using the average values from a time series graph and moving ranges, *i.e.*, the differences between contiguous individual values of the time series). They are based on the concept of "3 sigma," sigma being a measure of the spread of data around an average value. For further information on 3 sigma and control charts in general, see Don Wheeler's unrivaled explanations in *Understanding Statistical Process Control*, SPC Press 1992.)

In Figure A.1, we can see a control chart that contains data regarding the percentage of on time shipments made by a manufacturing company between January and May.

This chart shows a process which is likely to be statistically predictable in its evolution ("in control") because none of the points of the chart are above the upper control limit or below the lower control limit. The importance of this graph is that, unless major changes occur in the execution of the shipment process, next month's percentage of on time shipments will be, approximately, between 63 and 81 percent.

Let's look now at a chart (Figure A.2) related to the process of accumulation of work in progress in the same company we looked at before.

This figure shows a process that is not predictable in its evolution over time (out of control); two points lie above the upper control limit, and more than eight consecutive points are below the average-central

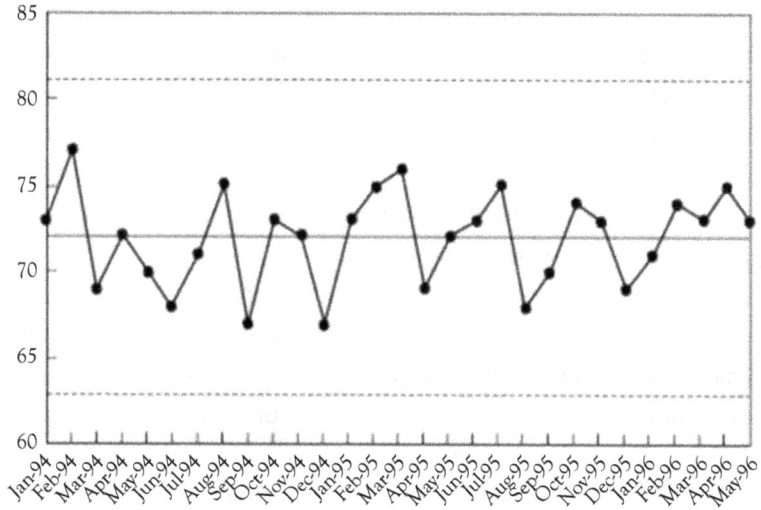

Figure A.1 A process that is in statistical control

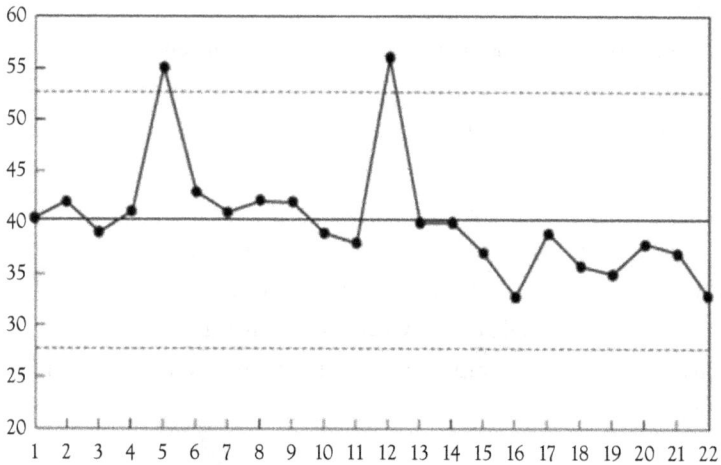

Figure A.2 A process that is not in statistical control

line. (The rules for detection of out-of-control processes can be found in Wheeler, *Understanding Statistical Process Control.*)

What can we say about this process? Not Much. Simply, we have no rational basis to predict how much work in progress we are going to have going forward.

Control charts are the tools that enable us to take meaningful actions. Depending on whether a process is in control or not, the action we take will differ radically. It is the manager's job to understand the kind of variation in the processes in order to take the appropriate actions to improve them.

We can use Deployment Flowcharts (DFC) to visualize the input-output network that defines our activities and to measure and improve the statistical predictability of the overall system by applying control charts to the main processes. Flowcharts allow us to to identify the best points for gathering data and building control charts.

According to Shewhart, the variation of a process can be either within limits or outside these limits: "While every process displays variation, some processes display controlled variation, while others display uncontrolled variation." Controlled variation is variation that is statistically stable hence consistent over time. It is due to *common causes*, causes which are intrinsically part of the process. A variation which is controlled makes the process predictable. Conversely, uncontrolled variation is not consistent over time. It is due to *special causes*, causes which are external to the process and its evolution is not predictable.

Executives must absolutely understand these concepts and make them the cornerstone of their decisions.

Failing to identify the source of variation, special or common, leads to taking inappropriate actions on the system that may worsen the situation. Deming called that "tampering with the system."

For Deming, the role of leadership is to pursue Quality by constantly reducing the sources of variation that undermine predictability, hence triggering what he called "The Chain Reaction": Improve Quality, costs decrease, productivity improves, capture the market, stay in business, provide jobs and more jobs.

To recap:

1. The data we need to analyze the system and support decision making must be presented in a suitable way.
2. The first problem to face in order to construct continuous improvement in our organizations is to understand the kind of variation which is affecting our processes.
3. The actions we take to improve our processes differ radically depending on the nature of the variation that affects them.

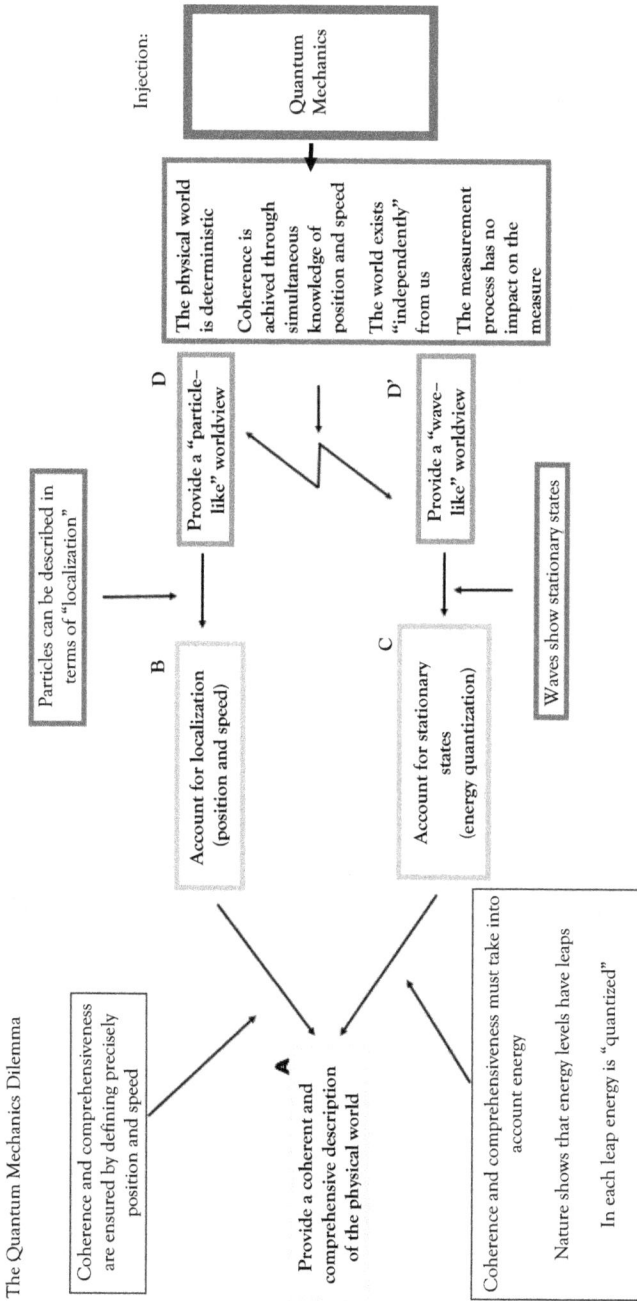

Figure A.3 *The "Quantum Mechanics conflict"*

The Dilemma of Quantum Mechanics

In our chapter for Springer called "Managing Complexity in Organizations Through a Systemic Network of Projects" (see Bibliography), we indulged in a cultural *divertissement* with the purpose of exemplifying how a breakthrough can be generated as a result of framing correctly conflicting positions, needs, goal, and assumptions. We picked one of the most revolutionary and paradigm-changing, seemingly unsolvable conflicts that arose at the beginning of the last century.

The "conflict" between particles and waves and the solution provided by Quantum Mechanics can be represented using the Conflict Cloud as we have done in Figure A.3; QM is what we could call "an Injection" to the dilemma of a "particle worldview" versus "wave worldview."

Bibliography

The following bibliography does not represent an exhaustive list of the resources that have been studied as part of the development of the work described in our book. This list does, however, provide a solid basis for an approach to all the aspects of systemic management.

Barabàsi, A. 2002. *Linked: the New Science of Networks*. Cambridge, MA: Perseus Publishing.

Barabàsi, A., and A. Reka. 1999. "Emergence of Scaling in Random Networks." *Science* 286, no. 5439, pp. 509–12.

Capra, F. 1996. *The Web of Life: A New Scientific Understanding of Living Systems*. New York, NY: Anchor Books.

Capra, F., and P.L. Luisi. 2014. *The Systems View of Life: A Unifying Vision*. Cambridge: Cambridge University Press.

Cialdini, R. 2006. *Influence*. New York, NY: Harper Business.

Corbett, T. 1998. *Throughput Accounting*. Great Barrington, MA: North River Press.

Deming, W.E. 1986. *Out of the Crisis*. Cambridge, MA: Massachusetts Institute of Technology. Center for Advanced Engineering Study.

Deming, W.E. 1993. *The New Economics for Industry, Government, Education*. Cambridge, MA: Massachusetts Institute of Technology Center for Advanced Engineering Study.

Deming of America. 1991. *(Documentary)*. Cincinnati, OH: The Petty Consulting/Productions.

Goldratt, E.M. 1984. *The Goal: A Process of Ongoing Improvement*. Great Barrington, MA: North River Press.

Goldratt, E.M. 1987. *The Theory of Constraints Journal*, Vols. 1–6. Avraham Goldratt Institute.

Goldratt, E.M. 1990. *The Haystack Syndrome: Sifting Information from the Data Ocean*. Great Barrington, MA: North River Press.

Goldratt, E.M. 1990. *What is this Thing Called the Theory of Constraints and How Should It Be Implemented?* Great Barrington, MA: North River Press.

Goldratt, E.M. 1994. *It's Not Luck*. Great Barrington, MA: North River Press.

Goldratt, E.M. 1997. *Critical Chain*. Great Barrington, MA: North River Press.

Goldratt, E.M. 1998. *Essays on the Theory of Constraints*. Great Barrington, MA: North River Press.

Kahneman, D., and A. Tverski. 2013. *Thinking Fast and Slow*. New York, NY: Farrar, Straus and Giroux.

Kahneman, D., P. Slovic, and A. Tverski, eds. 1982. *Judgement Under Uncertainty: Heuristics and Biases*. Cambridge: Cambridge University Press.

Killian, C.S. 1988. *The World of W. Edwards Deming*. Washington, DC: CEE Press.

Lepore, D. 2011. *Sechel: Logic, Language and Tools to Manage any Organization as a Network*. Toronto: Intelligent Management Inc.

Lepore, D., A. Montgomery, and G. Siepe. 2015. "Managing Complexity in Organizations Through a Systemic Network of Projects." In *Applications of Systems Thinking and Soft Operations Research in Managing Complexity*, ed. A. Masys, 35–69. Switzerland: Springer International Publishing.

Lepore, D., A. Montgomery, and G. Siepe. 2016. *Quality, Involvement, Flow: The Systemic Organization*. New York, NY: CRC Press.

Lepore, D., and O. Cohen. 1999. *Deming and Goldratt: The Decalogue*. Great Barrington, MA: North River Press.

Maci, G., D. Lepore, S. Pagano, and G. Siepe. 2008. *Systemic Approach to Management: A Case Study*. Poster presented at 5th European Conference on Complex Systems, Hebrew University, Givat Ram Campus, Jerusalem, Israel.

Maci, G., D. Lepore, S. Pagano, and G. Siepe. June 23–27, 2008. *Managing Organizations as a System: The Novamerican Case Study*. Poster presented at International Workshop and Conference on Network Science, Norwich Research Park, UK.

Mandelbrot, B. 1982. *The Fractal Geometry of Nature*. New York, NY: W.H. Freeman.

Mandelbrot, B., and R.L. Hudson. 2004. *The Misbehavior of Markets: A Fractal View of Financial Turbulence*. New York, NY: Basic Books.

Montgomery, A. 2015. *The Human Constraint*. Digital Business Novel and Online Knowledge Base published by Intelligent Management Inc.

Neave, H. 1990. *The Deming Dimension*. Knoxville, TN: SPC Press.

Schneerson, M.M. 1998. *On the Essence of Chassidus*. Brooklyn, NY: Kehot Publication Society.

Shewhart, W.A. 1931. *Economic Control of Quality of Manufactured Product*. New York, van Nostrand Company Inc.

Shewhart, W.A. 1986. *Statistical Method from the Viewpoint of Quality Control*, ed. W.E. Deming. Mineola, New York, NY: Dover.

Watt, D.J., and S. Strogatz. 1998. "Collective Dynamics of 'Small World' Networks." *Nature* 39, pp. 440–42.

Wheeler, D.J. 1983. *Four Possibilities*. Knoxville, TN: SPC Press.

Wheeler, D.J. 1992. *Understanding Statistical Process Control*. Knoxville, TN: SPC Press.

Wheeler, D.J. 1993. *Understanding Variation*. Knoxville, TN: SPC Press.

Wheeler, D.J. 1995. *Advanced Topics in Statistical Process Control*. Knoxville, TN: SPC Press.

Wheeler, D.J. 1998. *Avoiding Manmade Chaos*. Knoxville, TN: SPC Press.

Wheeler, D.J. 1998. *Building Continual Improvement*. Knoxville, TN: SPC Press.

Winograd, T., and F. Flores. 1987. *Understanding Computers and Cognition*. Boston , MA: Addison Wesley.

About the Author

With a background in solid-state physics and nonlinear dynamics, **Dr. Domenico Lepore** is an international expert and innovator in the application of science to management to radically improve business performance and achieve robust, predictable, and repeatable results.

Domenico has advised CEOs and decision makers internationally for over 20 years and has led implementations with his Decalogue management methodology at over 30 national and multinational organizations in a wide variety of industries, from mining to IT. This work included in the early 2000s the turnaround of a failing American multinational that adopted his methodology at a global level over a 3-year period to achieve measurable results in increased productivity, unleashing of untapped capacity, award-winning patents, and a stock price that increased in value sevenfold.

Domenico founded his first consulting firm in Milan, Italy, in 1996 where he developed his Decalogue methodology that uniquely combines the teachings of W. Edwards Deming with the practical applications from the Theory of Constraints. Thanks to the turnaround results achieved, he was invited to relocate to New York in 2006 to join a firm that successfully raised almost $600m to acquire and integrate a network of 22 facilities into one whole system. In 2010, he founded Intelligent Management Inc. with his partners Dr. Angela Montgomery and Dr. Giovanni Siepe in Toronto to help organizations evolve toward a network and system-based perspective for 21st century needs (www.intelligentmanagement.ws).

Together with a talented team of mathematicians and developers, Domenico's firm Intelligent Management created the first Project Management software to combine Critical Chain with Statistical Process Control to schedule competencies, not just resources, at finite capacity. See www.ess3ntial.com/

Domenico's first book, *Deming and Goldratt: The Decalogue* (1999), co-authored with Oded Cohen, was the first book to be published by Goldratt's publisher North River Press not authored by Goldratt himself.

It became recommended reading in universities around the world and was translated into several languages. His most recent book, co-authored with his partners at Intelligent Management Inc., is *Quality, Involvement, Flow: The Systemic Organization,* CRC Press, NYC, 2016.

A new Canadian citizen, Domenico lives in Victoria, BC, with Angela, his British-Canadian wife and partner. He travels regularly between North America and Europe to visit clients and keep contact with his roots and passion for international cinema and Italian cuisine.

Index

OTHER TITLES IN OUR SUPPLY AND OPERATIONS MANAGEMENT COLLECTION

Joy M. Field, Boston College, Editor

- *Contemporary Issues in Supply Chain Management and Logistics* by Anthony M.Pagano and Mellissa Gyimah
- *Understanding the Complexity of Emergency Supply Chains* by Matt Shatzkin
- *Mastering Leadership Alignment: Linking Value Creation to Cash Flow* by Jahn Ballard and Andrew Bargerstock
- *Statistical Process Control for Managers, Second Edition* by Victor Sower
- *Sustainable Operations and Closed Loop Supply Chains, Second Edition* by Gilvan Souza
- *The High Cost of Low Prices: A Roadmap to Sustainable Prosperity* by David S. Jacoby
- *The Global Supply Chain and Risk Management* by Stuart Rosenberg
- *The New Age Urban Transportation Systems: Cases from Asian Economies, Volume I* by Sundaravalli Narayanaswami
- *The New Age Urban Transportation Systems: Cases from Asian Economies, Volume II* by Sundaravalli Narayanaswami

Announcing the Business Expert Press Digital Library

Concise e-books business students need for classroom and research

This book can also be purchased in an e-book collection by your library as

- a one-time purchase,
- that is owned forever,
- allows for simultaneous readers,
- has no restrictions on printing, and
- can be downloaded as PDFs from within the library community.

Our digital library collections are a great solution to beat the rising cost of textbooks. E-books can be loaded into their course management systems or onto students' e-book readers.
The **Business Expert Press** digital libraries are very affordable, with no obligation to buy in future years. For more information, please visit **www.businessexpertpress.com/librarians**. To set up a trial in the United States, please email **sales@businessexpertpress.com**.

www.ingramcontent.com/pod-product-compliance
Lightning Source LLC
Chambersburg PA
CBHW061310220326
41599CB00026B/4814